imagine 10 – RAPIDS 2.0

Delft University of Technology, Faculty of Architecture,
Chair of Design of Construction

imagine 10

SERIES EDITED BY
Ulrich Knaack
Tillmann Klein
Marcel Bilow

RAPIDS 2.0

Ulrich Knaack
Dennis de Witte
Alamir Mohsen
Oliver Tessmann
Marcel Bilow

nai010 publishers, Rotterdam 2016

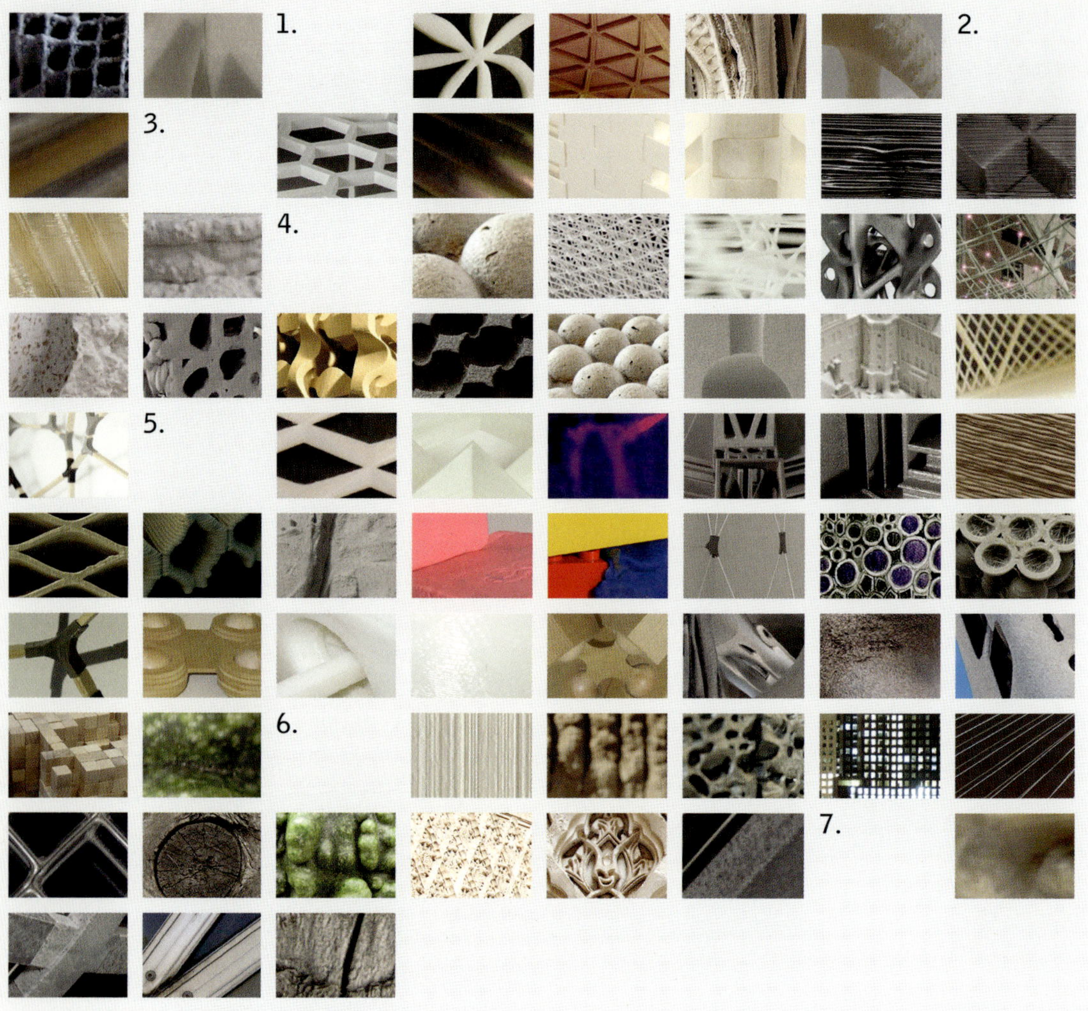

CONTENTS

chapter	page
FOREWORD	7
1. BRUTE-FORCE MATERIALIZATION	9
2. ADDITIVE MANUFACTURING (AM)	21
3. 3D PRINTING IS OUR FUTURE – REALLY?	31
4. AM SESSIONS	41
5. AM PROJECTS	65
6. AM EXPLORATIONS	99
7. WHAT A HYPE	115
APPENDIX	123
CVs	124
References	126
Credits	128

FOREWORD

The imagine series, developed at our faculty at TU Delft, is a book series championing ideas, concepts and physically built results. It is for designers and architects: to inspire them and to create a culture of imagination.
At the start, the editors needed to promise the publisher a series of ten books and started with imagine 01, "Façades", in 2008. The series continued with volumes about interesting ("Concretable", 08), relevant ("Energy", 05) and unusual aspects of architecture ("Deflate-ables", 02, which dealt with vacuum constructions, and "Rapids", 04, which took a first look into the world of additive manufacturing for buildings, something we now call 3D-printing).

Now, with number 10 we have completed the cycle. It is again about the development and the potentials of additive manufacturing for the built environment. This technology is developing very rapidly and promises to be revolutionary for the construction of buildings. It has the potential to truly bring mass-customization on a detail level. And it is interesting to see how imagine 04, "Rapids", helped to accelerate this development – some of the ideas mentioned in that issue felt really naive and impossible at the time. Today, a few years later, our colleagues at MIT refer to these books and are now printing with glass! This is what the book series was meant to do: to showcase potentials and to imagine possibilities.

Of course, the question now is how to continue? What are the next drivers and challenges? How will we be able to identify them, elaborate on them and convey the results to the right people? At the Faculty of Architecture and the Built Environment at TU Delft, we will focus in the coming years on the themes of AUTOMATION, in which the "rapid" fits perfectly by being about automated production; AFRICA, with the question of how to build capacity there; and AGILITY in education, which is what the books are about in the end, coming from our education and research environment.
It will be exciting to see how the editors react to these topics and shape the structure of the books to adapt to a new set of challenges. Now is the time for the Future!

Prof. Peter Russell
Dean of the Faculty of Architecture and the Built Environment, TU Delft

1. BRUTE-FORCE MATERIALIZATION

ABSTRACT

When looking at 3D printing as an isolated technology, material is placed tiny layer by tiny layer following the g-code of a digital model sliced with brute force. The process, expensive in time and cost, seems of little relevance for the scale of architectural construction. Well-established technologies are faster and less costly. As soon as Additive Manufacturing (AM) is embedded into a newly conceived process from design to materialization, however, the potentials for architecture beyond mere geometrical exuberance start to unfold. This text looks at what got lost through modernism and the industrialization of building, and subsequently examines projects and case studies that use AM within a design process that challenges 20th-century notions of architecture. The examples are just starting points for further research in novel digital process chains in architectural design and hint towards novel spaces, constructions and materials.

Pietro Belluschi and Pier Luigi Nervi, Cathedral of St. Mary of the Assumption, San Francisco 1971

INTRODUCTION

In computer science, the brute-force method solves algorithmic problems by systematically crawling through a solution space and checking all of its members as to whether they satisfy the problem's statement. Brute-force attacks on encrypted data, for example, systematically check all possible keys, starting with one-digit passwords before moving on to two-digit/three-digit/… passwords until the correct one is found. What's brute about the method is that there is no strategy involved beyond blunt number crunching. No prior analysis or heuristics are used to narrow down the solution space. However, if there is a solution the brute-force method will always find it, it is just a matter of time and the dimensions of a solution space.

When we 3D print an object we slice it into thousands of horizontal layers because we know that it works with every solid object. Every slice consists of at least one area-enclosing polygon that separates inside from outside, mass from void, bound material from loose material. 3D printing is the brute-force way of materializing. It slowly follows one simple rule and systematically builds up form layer by layer. No shortcuts possible.

MODERNISM ERASED COMPLEXITY

Just as the elegance of encryption algorithms is contrasted with the number crunching of brute-force attacks, 3D printing of objects significantly contrasts the way we can generate them in computational design processes. Aside from the technical challenges of depositing precise subsequent horizontal layers of plastics, concrete, steel, ceramics, binder etc. and creating bonds in between them, the act of 3D printing relies on the most simple and common denominator: slicing 3D geometry. "The 3-axis layer-based paradigm of conventional printing" (Tam, Coleman, Fine & Mueller, 2015). produces anisotropic materials systems in which the anisotropy is derived from the materialization process and is not driven by the structural need of a construction element. The process destroys information, generated and gathered in the design process, instead of informing the printed object.

The fact that production processes define the form and performance of construction elements is well known from the industrial age. The way building components look and perform and the amount of material they consume today is not only defined by the requirements they are exposed to as a part of a building but also by the way they are produced. Industrial serial production and increasing labor costs are the economic drivers of form. Every subtractive activity such as milling or drilling and every act of connecting and assembling elements like welding comes with a price tag of a scale that makes material consumption economically irrelevant; working hours count. For Konrad Wachsmann it was mass production that discriminated industrialization from craftsmanship. Not the produced object is the original, but the tool that produces the object or the mold that forms it, becomes the original. The serial products are mere derivatives without any individual traces of their becoming (Wachsmann, 1959). Wachsmann's conceptual shift from craft to industry was a necessary and logical step in the middle of the 20th century and it paved the way for novel systems and typologies. However it made production techniques define product typologies, which led to construction typologies that crept into the design thinking of architects and engineers. Today pre-fabricated concrete elements such as columns and beams are not sized according to the local stresses they are exposed to in the construction but rather by the structural elements that receive the highest loads in the construction. Thus, many columns and beams, all fabricated from the same formwork, consume more material than they need to perform structurally. Differentiation is prohibited by the production technique. Rare examples, such as the work of Pier Luigi Nervi, show the structural but also architectural and aesthetic potential of such a differentiation. Nervi's rip structures follow the trajectories of principal stress patterns in the material and at the same time become an ornament.

COMPUTATIONAL COMPLEXITY

The newly awakened interest in Nervi's work in the age of computational design can be explained by an interest in its "topologically deforming pattern in order to accommodate the differential behaviors of structures" (Zaera-Polo, 2009), but more important is the approach to closely link analysis to synthesis. Stress patterns and load-paths become design features rather than problems to overcome. To materialize these patterns is fundamentally different from merely analyzing them.

Today computation allows us to merge generative and analytical processes within one design environment. Structural analysis, form-finding, evolutionary optimization, daylight and acoustical simulation, previously hidden away from designers in expert systems, become accessible as digital tools and design drivers (Peters, 2013). Form is not merely geometrical representation but instantly becomes the subject of structural, material or environmental analysis. Performance is simulated and the results of such simulations are fed back into the generative design process to allow for iterative improvement through feedback loops. Form can thus be optimized for single criteria or, what is more relevant in architecture, put into a state that balances and negotiates the various requirements of an architectural component or even the entire building. Computation helps us to design, control and represent such complex systems and their intricate internal relationships. Instead of collaging recognizable objects together, computational design supports us in our search for coherent systems that rely on ratios and relations rather than compositions (Reiser & Umemoto, 2006). The differentiated results of such an integrative design process, however, need to be materialized accordingly. The above-described industrial processes of mass production are not capable of providing variation within the pre-fabrication of building elements. Craftsmanship would neither be affordable nor able to handle the scale of the necessary production today. Thus we are still experiencing a gap between what we are able to design and what we are able to materialize. Through digital fabrication architects have come a long way in their ambition to materialize the computationally designed buildings and structures. However, many of the realized projects focus on transferring the formal aspects of geometrical complexity from the digital into the physical through mostly subtractive methods. Computation, however, can provide more than formally expressive buildings. Linking synthesis to analysis informs geometry beyond mere aesthetics.

COMPLEXITY IN DESIGN VS. SIMPLICITY IN THE MATERIALIZATION

Today we are experiencing the slow migration of Additive Manufacturing into the construction industry. Limited dimensions of 3D printers and only partially explored and standardized material properties give architects a little more time to reflect on the role of the, not so new, technology in their discipline. 3D printing is, for better or worse, tied to a digital form generation process. Only digital models can be transformed into a stack of closed contours that are subsequently materialized. The very controlled deposition of material, the additive approach of 3D printing, creates a strong conceptual link to the above described computational design approaches. Form is differentiated and emerges out of a process that makes local structural, environmental and contextual boundary conditions the driving forces of the shape, strength and porosity of a building component. AM is the technology that provides the means to materialize those ambitious design concepts. Integrating AM into a digital process chain from ideation to materialization will generate repercussions in both directions: the way we design will require the fabrication technology to evolve while the provided technologies challenge existing notions of form generation.

TOPOLOGY OPTIMIZATION AND AM

Complexity comes for free with 3D printing is a common saying. What is meant is that the level of geometric complexity of an object has no impact on the slicing and the additive process. Printing time and material consumption are mostly defined by the volume that gets printed but not by its shape. Form is not the driver of production cost anymore. This gives architects the chance to reconsider and question established construction typologies. Why are things designed the way they are? Why do components look the way they look?

If we don't want to merely create geometric complexity for the sake of complexity, we have to understand why we need it and how we can achieve it. Topology optimization is a computational form generation strategy that congenially complements the materialization through 3D printing. It allows for a material distribution according to structural needs. Material is placed where it is needed to transfer loads. The iterative computational form generation process starts with the definition of a maximum spatial envelope of an object. The inner volume of the envelope is subdivided into voxels (3D pixels). Furthermore supports and loads are defined. In a digital simulation the volume is exposed to external loads that need to be transferred into the supports. The system calculates the load paths and stress distribution within the volume. Simply speaking, voxels that are not exposed to external loads are removed from the volume while the ones that transfer loads remain. After several iterations the volume in the envelope is reduced to the zones that are responsible for load transfer. Depending on the boundary condition of loads and supports the emerging topology is of high complexity. The generated structures resemble naturally grown structures.

In 1917, D'Arcy Thompson showed sections of human bones in his seminal publication *On Growth and Form*. In the book he explains that in nature form and force flow cannot be seen as two separated elements but rather as two components of the same thing. The form of an object is its force diagram, which displays the forces that have been at work during its morphogenesis. The topology of bone tissue, composed of microscopic beams, struts and rods called trabeculae, is a good example for Thompson's thesis: the trabeculae consist of patterns that

1 Additive Manufactured steel node by Arup
2 *Arabesque Wall* (2014/2015), image courtesy of Benjamin Dillenburger and Michael Hansmeyer
3 *Digital Grotesque* (2013), image courtesy of Benjamin Dillenburger and Michael Hansmeyer

look very similar to the trajectories engineers use to visualize force flow in a construction. Here form emerges out of a process of material allocation along load paths. D'Arcy Thompson tells the anecdote of Karl Culman, a famous engineer who developed the graphic static, being inspired by the cross section of a human bone he discovered in the medical labs of the university and how he migrated these patterns into the design of a crane.

Meanwhile architects like Hector Guimard, the designer of the entrance to the Porte Dauphine metro station in Paris 1912 and a famous representative of the Art Noveau style, used floral and natural forms as inspiration for decorative objects and reliefs in their designs.

But in 1912 the potential synergy of natural forms as "optimized" structures and their role as architectural ornamentation was not obvious. Modernism abandoned ornamentation in architecture and with it all references to natural morphogenesis. Building components such as structure, envelope, partition walls etc. were separated from each other rather than merged together.
More than a hundred years later Arup and Salomé Galjaard use Topology Optimization and Additive Manufacturing (AM) in 2014 to design a steel node that combines structural performance with ornamental quality. The team questions the design of conventional steel nodes for a tensegrity structure by migrating selective laser sintering into the construction industry.

Despite the fact that the technology is far from affordable for architecture, the engineers prototype a design to production process that links Topology Optimization to AM in a way that allows

for a novel confluence of aesthetic and structural performance. The steel node is one of 1200 different nodes within an irregular tensegrity structure. Every node is connected to various struts with different directions in space. Serial production is not an option for the highly differentiated geometry. Conventional customization of production through CNC cutting still requires labor intensive welding of the single parts. AM is the most convincing approach to tackle the geometric differentiation of the design. The resulting steel node has very little in common with the conventional one. While the latter consists of a tube and six welded steel plates – elements that are easy to manufacture – the form of the AM node is exclusively driven by the loads and their directions at the particular location of the node in the tensegrity structure (Ren & Galjaard, 2015). The topology resembles natural grown structures with the most efficient load path. The design team describes Topology Optimization as a well-known and widely implemented design tool but they also describe the necessary refinement of the coarse geometry yielded by the optimization procedure (Ren & Galjaard, 2015). It was only after a "design interpretation" (Ren & Galjaard, 2015) that included surface smoothing, that the final geometry was printed. The case study shows that many techniques and technologies are available on the way from ideation to final product. However, connecting these island solutions to form a design process is a challenge and a task for designers and engineers today. The project exemplifies a very consistent design to production process. Both Topology Optimization and AM unfold their full potential through a consistent workflow. The geometry, resulting from the design process, doesn't need to be rationalized according to fabrication constraints and the potential to effortlessly produce intricate geometry through AM is fully exploited. (see also page 50)

In the near future we will witness AM developing an increase in scale and material diversity, in parallel with a decrease in production costs. Architects and artists have started exploring these potentials. The work of Michael Hansmeyer and Benjamin Dillenburger aims at scaling 3D print towards the architectural scale by printing massive and highly complex architectural objects. Their grotesque sculptures carry names that refer to architectural elements such as "Arabesque Wall" and "Columns". Their design techniques and production technology inform and challenge each other in both directions. To fully exploit the 0.2 mm layer resolution of the sand printers 200 million surfaces and 50 GB production data has to be algorithmically tackled by the digital design tool (Hansmeyer, 2016). The exuberant artistic and architectural installations challenge formal categories and explore novel forms rather than improving existing ones. AM technologies open up a field of form exploration that has not existed before. Instead of erasing details Hansmeyer and Dillenburger would like to develop digital models with a resolution similar to the grain of sand they print with (Peters, 2015).

Philippe Morel and his Studio EZCT Architecture & Design Research in Paris print sand forms as formwork for Ultra High Performance Concrete (UHPC). The concrete is exclusively made from extremely fine aggregates, which leads to unprecedented rheology. With the improved flow properties of concrete, formwork can become geometrically more complex as the material reaches every cavity of the mold.

UHPC has material proporties and a structural performance that position the material somewhere between steel and conventional concrete. Forms and structural typologies previously only buildable with steel can be made from concrete. Philippe Morel and his team hence propose concrete space frames, molded into 3D printed formwork (Morel, n.d.). Here AM is used in the context of a traditional construction material that experienced innovation through material science.

The three case studies use AM to challenge architecture and construction in different ways. The AM node reveals how strongly our construction elements are constrained by conventional and subtractive production technologies and assembly procedures. If we don't question these traditions and develop novel design processes the potential of AM will never be fully exploited. Hansmeyer's and Dillenburger's innovation is a spatial and artistic one that requires software development to control form generation at the scale of the smallest building block, the grain of sand. Philippe Morel and his team reveal the full potential of UHPC by developing novel formwork production techniques. In all examples AM is never treated as an isolated technology that only replaces a conventional materialization procedure within an otherwise unaltered design to production process. The projects are fundamentally different from recent proposals to 3D print vertical concrete walls in the way they thoughtfully weave AM into a novel design process.

The way we build today might be said to lack innovation. However, many materialization and construction procedures have been widely tested and are well established. Their efficiency in cost and speed can hardly be challenged by AM today. What AM can challenge though are unquestioned and unthoughtfully accepted conventions and typologies that developed out of architectural history and the limitations of conventional fabrication.

The separation between designing and making is a 500-year long tradition begun during the Renaissance. The abstraction of a scaled drawing and parallel projection favors certain geometries over others in the design process (Carpo, 2011). Digital models create a much smoother link between the idea and the physical object. The mechanical notion of space, structure and construction as proposed by modernism excludes forms that structurally perform better than orthogonally organized building blocks and spaces that are much richer than the white cube.

The decomposition of buildings and building facades into various layers with a single functionality de-composes complex problems into less complex sub-problems that are solved in isolation and re-composed afterwards; a process that is coupled to the aspiration that the (re-)assembly performs as a system (Fischer, 2008, p. 38).
With this approach, facades delaminate into multiple layers of different functionality, mechanical systems of buildings live a life of their own (Reyner Banham, 1969), penetrating structure and space defining elements, and load bearing is dissociated from enveloping. The obvious benefits of independent subsystems come with the cost of increased material consumption and a fragmentation of the design process into islands of expertise with, sometimes, poor connectivity.

Konrad Wachsmann's ideas about the industrialization of building and the inherent idea of mass production have been overcome by mass customization and digital fabrication. Stepping from subtractive to additive manufacturing poses novel challenges and opportunities as presented above.

IF WE CAN PLACE MATERIAL WHEREVER WE WANT, WHERE DO WE PLACE IT?

This decision can be driven by structural considerations as shown in the example of the AM node by Arup. It can be driven by the aim to increase the resolution, and with it, the complexity of architectural volumes and surfaces as in the work of Hansmeyer and Dillenburger. It can reveal the potentials of another material such as UHPC.

Designing on the scale of a grain of sand connects architectural design with material design. Such a scale opens up a whole novel universe of opportunities for architects.
Constructions can be integrated and monolithic while responding to the various architectural and technical requirements of a structure and an envelope. Gradually changing material densities allow building components to perform differently in different regions, from load bearing to insulating to humidity regulating. Porosity is not the result of a chemical process but is rather controlled through voxels in the digital model. As we have experienced analysis and simulation migrating into our modeling tools, we might see material property design become another layer of information in the digital design models.

AM will interface with existing construction technologies and has to find its niche within the process of building.

Thus context-sensitive 3D printing beyond the allocation of material on a perfectly horizontal build plate is a necessary next step in the development of the technology. In combination with 3D scanning, such an approach could allow AM to leave prefabrication behind and enter the construction sites. Reality computing, the process of capturing the as-built with technologies such as laser scanning and photogrammetry and representing the information in the digital model as point clouds, can be a starting point for new additions of material intricately linked to the already existing.

The improvement of printable materials, their simulation in digital models and robotic fabrication pave the way to additive manufacturing procedures that might leave the brute-force approach of placing material in horizontal layers behind. The current anisotropy of 3D printed objects results from these layers. Potential delamination weakens 3D printed objects in one direction. If AM combines the layering technique with procedures that relate to extrusion and pultrusion, anisotropy will become a design feature rather than a trace of materialization. Future innovations require interdisciplinary cooperation. We have to innovate the entire design process from ideation, to digital modeling to materialization.

2. ADDITIVE MANUFACTURING (AM): A DESCRIPTION OF THE TECHNOLOGY

Additive Manufacturing is a process that is steered and controlled by the power of virtual 3D CAD data.

Additive Manufacturing or what is commonly known as 3D printing is a technology still trying to reach the maturity phase. The process receives both positive and sceptical feedback but the truth actually lies somewhere in between.

The early beginnings of Additive Manufacturing took place in the 1980s. Hideo Kodama of the Nagoya Municipal Industrial Research Institute invented a machine that created 3D objects with photo-hardening polymer, whereby the requested layer was exposed to UV light. Then in 1983, the American Chuck Hull of 3D Systems Corporation developed a prototype based on a process called Stereolithography, whereby photopolymers were cured with ultraviolet light lasers.

Beginning at the turn of the millennium, Additive Manufacturing experienced a boom and became a subject undergoing intense study in terms of what it could offer to the manufacture of complex geometries, which traditional manufacturing methods failed to achieve.

Nowadays there are several techniques for generating complex three-dimensional objects; thus Additive Manufacturing is scientifically used to describe any of these techniques such as extrusion and sintering-based processes. Each technique is characterized by its own limitations and capabilities, which should be accurately observed to accommodate the purpose and usage of the printed piece.

Additive Manufacturing offers the use of different materials such as plastics, metals, ceramics, etc. The choice of material is strongly connected with the applied technology as some machines are suited to printing certain kinds of materials but not others.

Based on the theory that any geometrical form can be rebuilt by transforming the targeted geometry to a sequence of contoured layers, which could be equal in thicknesses or different based on other factors, the process can be broken down into certain steps, which represents almost all AM technologies:

a. Creating a digital model, which defines the geometry's external surface.
b. Transforming the targeted model to STL format; this is generally suitable for nearly all AM technologies.
c. Transforming the STL file to match the 3D printer in use; considering that each 3D printer may have its own way to manipulate the digital data and generating the appropriate G-code needed to run the 3D printer.
d. The printing process starts after receiving the required data provided by the process mentioned earlier.
e. Creating the final model, which in certain cases will require going through final post-processing stages to finalize and prepare the model for end-use.

CATEGORIZATION

AM technologies differ based on the method of creating the layers, the way they process the bonding phase and the type of source material.
For example, Selective Laser Melting (SLM), Direct Metal Laser Sintering (DMLS), Selective Laser Sintering (SLS), Fused Deposition Modeling (FDM) and Fused Filament Fabrication (FFF) are techniques that have many similarities

regarding the basics of the printing process. On the other hand, there are other techniques, which utilize more sophisticated methods, such as Stereolithography (SLA), as it cures the printed layers of liquid resin by exposing the resin to UV rays. Another technique is Laminated Object Manufacturing (LOM), which works by cutting thin layers that are shaped and joined together to form the final model.

The main categories that are commonly used are as follows (illustrated on the next page):

A. Vat Photopolymerization

This technology is based on using a vat of liquid photopolymer resin; the model is basically constructed by selective solidification of the liquid resin using ultraviolet (UV) light.

The main two technologies following this theory are Stereolithography (SLA) and Digital Light Processing (DLP).

This is the oldest additive manufacturing technology and considered as the basis for the development of the other Additive Manufacturing techniques in general.

The photopolymer in its liquid state is used as the source for the printing material, and after being exposed to UV light it changes its properties and solidifies.

– Stereolithography (SLA)

The first use of Stereolithography was by Chuck Hull in 1984.

The process is based on the use of photopolymer resin, which solidifies when exposed to a laser ray. The layer thicknesses are between 0.05 and 0.25 mm, and in micro-stereolithography layer thicknesses of 0.001 mm can be achieved.

The sequence of the printing process starts with depositing the resin, lowering the build plate by the required layer thickness, then the UV light cures the resin layer by layer until the whole model is printed. As a final step the remaining resin is drained and the printed piece is removed and post-processed.

The printed elements are characterized by high accuracy and a smooth surface but the resin is relatively expensive in comparison with other materials, in addition to the limitation of using photo resins.

– Digital Light Processing (DLP)

This process is very similar to Stereolithography. It was first introduced in 1987 by Larry Hornbeck of Texas Instruments; it consists of a display device based on a digital micro mirror laid out on a semiconductor chip, which is suitable for projector devices as well as 3D printing.

The technology exploits the micro mirror, which projects a certain grid of rays based on the printed piece resolution.

The intensity of the projected rays can be controlled; accordingly, different properties for the printed elements can be applied.

The build plate moves upward to allow the next printed layer to be printed. The technology has an excellent resolution, leaves less waste material and is faster than SLA.

The source material is a liquid plastic resin in a transparent resin container.

B. Binder Jetting, 3D Printing (3DP)

This technology is much like ink-jet printing and was first developed in 1993 by the Massachusetts Institute of Technology. In 1995, Z Corporation – owned by 3D Systems – obtained an exclusive license.

The technology involves two different materials – a powder based material and a binder material. A roller is used to spread the powder material with the required layer thickness, then the binder material is laid on top of the powder forming the required base for the next

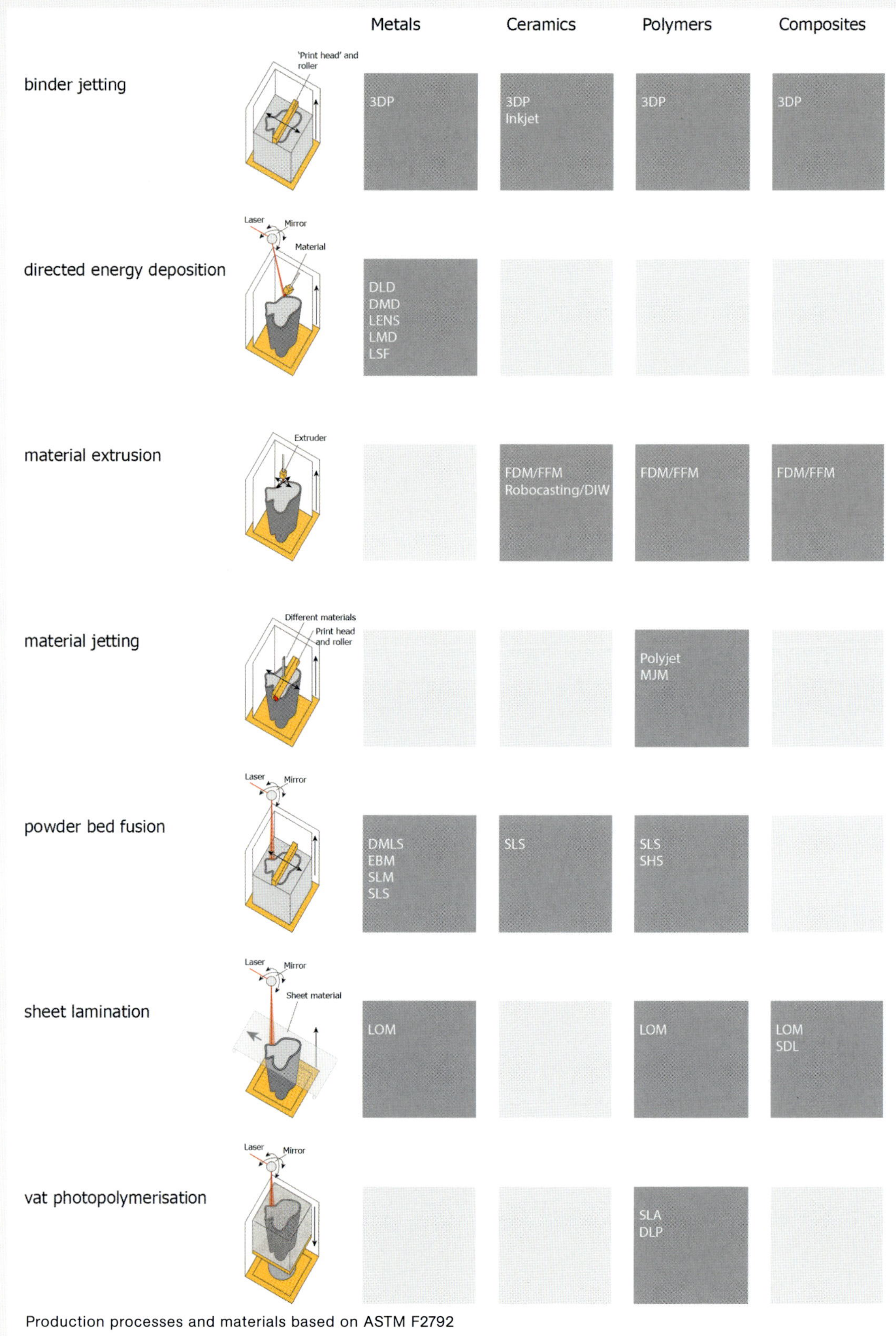

		Metals	Ceramics	Polymers	Composites
binder jetting		3DP	3DP Inkjet	3DP	3DP
directed energy deposition		DLD DMD LENS LMD LSF			
material extrusion			FDM/FFM Robocasting/DIW	FDM/FFM	FDM/FFM
material jetting				Polyjet MJM	
powder bed fusion		DMLS EBM SLM SLS	SLS	SLS SHS	
sheet lamination		LOM		LOM	LOM SDL
vat photopolymerisation				SLA DLP	

Production processes and materials based on ASTM F2792

layer. The build plate is then lowered to allow the process to repeat.

The technology makes it possible to print full color objects, for example printing models that represent FEM results. Mostly, the printed models do not have excellent mechanical properties and have to be infiltrated by melted wax, cyanoacrylate glue, epoxy, etc. to gain more structural stability.

There is a wide range of materials available that can be used with this technology such as different plastic powders, metals and ceramics. The main advantages of using the technology lies in the lower printing cost and the printing speed reaching up to 20 mm per hour. The accuracy of the printed pieces is relatively good as the minimum layer thickness is c. 0.1 mm. The use of support structures is usually not needed as the non-solidified powder acts as support material and can be reused. The technology is truly effective in printing positive molds, and allows for a wide range of applications to be utilized.

C. Material Extrusion

Material Extrusion is considered one of the most utilized techniques for Additive Manufacturing for personal 3D printers. The process is based on using (heated) extruders, to which the source material is fed to print the model in the form of a filament or ink composition. The extruders move in the x and y directions and the build plate moves in the z direction.

There is a great variety of filaments and ink compositions available; characterized by different properties to enhance the final product properties.

adopted the same technology. One of them was Makerbot who named the process Fused Filament Fabrication (FFF). The technology offers the printing of functional prototypes as well as concept models. Layer thickness ranges between 0.10 mm and 0.25 mm, depending on the machine. The printed model can be broken down to shells – the outer layer of the model – and infill – the inner pattern. The minimum thickness of the shells varies according to the material used as it ensures the stability of the models. There are some challenges with these machines such as calibration problems and clogging of the nozzle. Another issue is the difficulty to control the extruder's temperature precisely, which may cause defects in the printed models in the event of under-extrusion. The complexity of the printed models is limited to a certain extent, and to get the most out of the technology printing supports are commonly applied, which widen the possibility to print more complex elements; but on the other hand printing the supports may affect the smoothness of the model surface because the supports need to be broken off.

Different printing room sizes are offered, depending on the machine. The most common size is X/Y/Z = 300 x 200 x 250 mm but bigger sizes are offered as well, for example the 3D printer by BigRep, which has a building room of X/Y/Z = 1100 x 1067 x 1097 mm.

A wide variety of plastic filaments with different properties are available as well as carbon fiber, ceramic and wood filaments.

– Fused Deposition Modeling (FDM), Fused Filament Fabrication (FFF)

Fused Deposition Modeling (FDM) was invented by Scott Crump, the founder of Stratasys Ltd in the 1980s. After the patent of the system expired, other companies

– Robocasting or Direct Ink Writing (DIW)

The principle is much like Fused Deposition Modeling (FDM) but different in the form of the material used as it is basically ceramic slurry referred to as ink, which is extruded through a nozzle to form the printed layers.

The parts are usually very fragile and soft until dried and fired to achieve the desired mechanical properties.

D. Powder Bed Fusion

Powder Bed Fusion involves selective melting and re-solidification of powders. When plastic-based powders are used no support materials need to be added as the powder acts as support material for the printed layers. On the other hand, metal powders need supports to avoid warping. A layer of powder is deposited, and a laser or electron beam fuses the layers based on the contour data forming the final model.

Direct Metal Laser Sintering (DMLS), Electron Beam Melting (EBM), Selective Heat Sintering (SHS), Selective Laser Sintering (SLS) and Selective Laser Melting (SLM) are the main common techniques for powder bed fusion processes.

– Selective Laser Sintering (SLS)

This technology was developed by Dr. Carl Deckard and Dr. Joseph Beaman from the University of Texas in the mid 1980s.

The machines consist of three main components: a heat source (laser) to fuse the material, a mechanism to control the heating process and another mechanism to control adding new layers.

Basically, the three following aspects define which kind of sintering is applied:

- Solid state sintering, where the material stays in the solid state and forms the binding reaction only through heating the particles.
- Chemically induced binding, where an additional gluing material under heating conditions performs the binding process.
- Liquid phase sintering, where the particles partly melt to allow the binding process to emanate.

The powder used for printing may contain a binding agent, or the powder material itself is capable of binding through the sintering process.

The technology is fast as the laser only melts the outer surface of the particles to induce the fusing process between the solid non-melted cores to each other and to the layer below, which introduces a disadvantage as the printed model is not homogeneous and watertightness is not always achievable.

A special SLS technique uses micro laser sintering, achieving layer thicknesses between 1 μm and 5 μm.

– Selective Laser Melting (SLM)

Selective Laser Melting (SLM) started as a German research project at the Fraunhofer Institute in 1995.

The technology follows the same principle as selective laser sintering with the difference that the material is completely melted down by the laser source, resulting in the great advantage that the printed parts are homogeneous.

A wide variety of alloys can be used as print material. The print of fine structures is possible but support structures have to be considered, since the inherent high temperatures can cause warpage.

The disadvantage of this technology is the slow printing process as the density of the printed part increases simultaneously with the increase in energy density.

– Selective Heat Sintering (SHS)

Selective Heat Sintering is a 3D printing process, which follows the same rules as Selective Laser Sintering in a more simplified way.

More binding material is used, which either gets mixed with the printing powder through melting or is used to envelop the powder particles to form the final material.

The main advantage of this process is that the heating source is simpler than with the other technologies, e.g. a simple electric arc.

The first to offer this technology was the company Blueprinter to fulfill its goal of offering a low cost 3D printer. The company exchanged the expensive laser used in sintering 3D printers with a thermal print head that applies heat on layers of thermoplastic powder in a build chamber.

This technology can print layer thicknesses of 1 mm; the unused powder acts as a support material and can be reused.

– Electron Beam Melting (EBM)

The EBM technology works in the same way as SLS and SLM but the heating source used is a high power electron beam that is controlled by electromagnetic coils; thus the mechanical properties of the materials stay unaffected.

The building environment is set under strong vacuum, which is very advantageous in terms of the generated material's homogeneity, but also poses a limitation on printing size.

E. Sheet Lamination

Sheet Lamination is described as Laminated Object Manufacturing (LOM) or Selective Deposition Lamination (SDL). This is a process where prefabricated foils or sheets are used as print material, and a knife or laser cutter is used to form the required shape. The layers are then bonded with glue in the case of paper and plastic and ultrasonic welding in the case of metals.

– Laminated Object Manufacturing (LOM)

The first LOM system was developed by Helisys, Inc in 2000. The idea was to use materials such as paper, plastic or metal in sheet form. Rolling blades feed the sheets to the build plate and then a cutting blade cuts out the desired shape. The process is repeated for each additional layer until the model is complete.

When paper or plastic is used as print material, it gets bonded with an adhesive or laminated using heat and pressure. When metal sheets are used, ultrasonic welding is used to bond the layers together.

This technology is considered a low cost alternative, and it has its limitation as the models produced do not have a great level of accuracy and complex geometries cannot be achieved.

– Selective Deposition Lamination (SDL)

This process was developed by Mcor Technologies. It uses only paper as print material – ordinary sheets of A4 and letter size paper. In contrast to LOM it adds the adhesive material with different densities to allow easy removal of the surrounding material of the printed model.

The build plate moves downward like other 3D printing techniques but the movement is interrupted by an upward movement to press the new layer so as to enable a complete bond.

A colored model is possible simply by printing the outline of the layers on the required papers before adding them to the printer and starting the printing process. The same limitations as with LOM apply, i.e. complex geometries and hollow objects are not possible and accuracy is rather low compared to other 3D printing techniques.

F. Material Jetting

Material Jetting is similar to normal inkjet printing and works by jetting drops of material to create a 3D object. The inkjet technology uses print heads to jet the liquid photopolymers or wax onto the build platform.

The technology of material jetting has been referred to by different names such as MultiJet Modeling (MJM) or Polyjet. After jetting the material onto the build plate, the material gets cured by UV. Printing support material and overhangs is possible; the completed model needs to be placed in a washing unit to dissolve the support material, which typically has different properties than the material that forms the model.

Material Jetting has many advantages over other technologies as it allows the printing of smooth and detailed prototypes, in addition to the ability to produce complex shapes.

Another advantage is the ability to print multiple materials simultaneously; thus controlling the colors and the mechanical properties of parts of the printed model is conceivable.

On the other hand, mixing too many materials with different properties might lead to printed models that are not very durable and exhibit limited mechanical properties.

G. Direct Energy Deposition

Direct Energy Deposition is a complex printing process that comprises many terms: "Electron Beam Additive Manufacturing (EBAM), Laser Engineered Net Shaping (LENS), Direct Metal Deposition (DMD) and Laser Metal Deposition (LMD)."

The process is mainly based on melting metals in powder or wire form with an electron beam, a laser or plasma arc onto a specific surface. Usually this process is used to repair existing expensive parts, which means that the printed part is added to an existing element.

The targeted part is fixed on a 4 or 5 axis build plate, and the print material is fed from 1, 2, 3 or 4 nozzles, according to the type of the machine used.

The process takes place in a vacuum environment and is very precise, as the deposition of a layer of the utilized material varies between 0.1 mm and several millimeters.

When a feed wire is used as print material, an inert gas shielding is incorporated.

ARUP, Amsterdam

DUS Architects, Amsterdam

Contour Crafting, University of
Southern California, Los Angeles

Holger Strauß, TU Delft, Delft   Winsum new materials, Shanghai

D-Shape, London

AM IN THE BUILT ENVIRONMENT

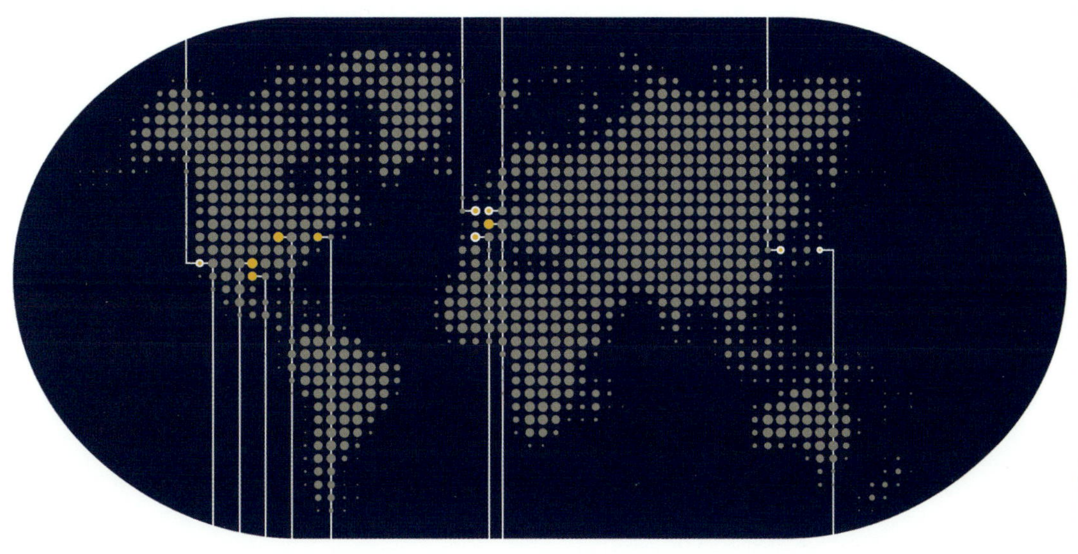

TECHNOLOGY

SLA - Chuck Hull, 3D
Systems, Los Angeles

3DP - MIT,
Massachusetts

SLM - Frauenhofer, Aachen

SLA - Hideo Kodama of
Nagoya Municipal Industrial
Research Institute, Nagoya

LOM - Helisys Inc,
Torrance

FDM - Scott Crump,
Stratasys, Edina

SLA - Alain Le Méhauté, Olivier de
Witte and Jean Claude André, French

SLS - Carl Deckard and Joe Beaman,
University of Texas, Austin

DLP - Larry Hornbeck,
Texas Instruments, Dallas

AM world map

3. 3D PRINTING IS OUR FUTURE – REALLY?

If we follow the press we cannot deny that 3D printing is the hottest topic ever and will change our world entirely. The technology also known as Additive Manufacturing (AM) or Rapid Prototyping is already more than three decades old. Three decades? Really? Yes, Chuck Hull experimented with UV solidified liquids with his stereolithographic processes as early as 1983 and the technology was patented a year later.

We don't want to rewrite the entire history of the development of this technology … this would take more pages than the entire book contains, but the fact that the first patents have already run out highlights the success story that we are witnessing now.

First of all, 3D printing is the fastest developing technology and the opportunities are endless. But that is exactly the challenge we now face – as architects and engineers we have to raise the question of how to apply these emerging technologies to our built environment.
In short: Are we really able to "print" our houses in the future?

Following the news carefully shows that there are houses already being printed all over the world, and the different approaches we see try to solve the overall challenge piece by piece. DUS Architects in Amsterdam with their 3D printed canal house focus on the possibilities of the freedom of design while using less suitable materials for their projects, and projects in China copy Prof. Khoshnevis's technologies and his Contour Crafting processes, producing concrete prefab elements with the focus on a fast and cheap method to build for the masses.
As architects we see the opportunity and the freedom that the digital production technologies offer: to build layer by layer entirely without the costs for casting systems or molds. Free form seems to have become more affordable and as easily built as designed due to the fact that a curved surface can be printed as easily as a straight box.
But hold on; how close are we to realizing the dream of printing houses? Additive Manufacturing technologies are already widely spread in all kinds of industries. Tooth prosthetics and hearing aid devices are often produced with AM technologies. Dentists do not advertise that they use 3D printed teeth, it is just the best technology available to make the job better and easier. Formula 1 has been using 3D printed parts for a long time, to test and experiment with high performance parts for engines, exhausts and suspension systems; hunting for that split second to beat the competitors while budgets seem to be endless.

While the technologies and machines become so good and affordable to produce small sized dental prosthetics or hearing aids, Formula 1 is able to pay high prices for a single performance part knowing what it saves them as compared to the more classic methods of production.

In short it can be stated that we can already produce real products for our daily life made from a huge variety of materials as long as we are working within the building formats of a shoebox or two.
Of course a few of the existing technologies can be sized up easily; such as the KamerMaker developed by DUS Architects, an up-sized FDM printer which, in its original size, can be found in every fab lab, at universities and even in public libraries. While this technology relies on a low temperature melting polymer, it is obvious that the material

1 Flaws within the production technologies create
  a unique pattern (DUS Architects)
2-3 A 3D printed wall element (DUS Architects)
4 Inside the printing chamber (KamerMaker at
  DUS Architects)
5 A wall element with a gradient from opaque to
  translucent (DUS Architects)

properties will not fulfill the requirements in comparison to common building materials like wood, bricks or concrete. Therefore, wise design choices need to be made in terms of what will be needed in the future if more reliable building materials are available.

The materials that fulfill building requirements are incredibly expensive, and the machines with heated building chambers and powerful lasers cannot be scaled up easily. With the right applications 3D printed parts can be created in a couple of years that will be used in combination with standard components; these will be affordable due to the constantly decreasing cost of the technologies and the ability to reduce the amount of material used for the part itself by using form and shape optimizing algorithms. The team of Arup around Salomé Galjaard already showed some first promising details for node connections printed in steel and TU Delft's Facade Research Group introduced the development of a free-form facade mullion knot printed in aluminum years ago.

Additive Manufacturing will doubtlessly have a big influence on our built environment as well, evolving into one method with which we might build houses in the future. But honestly, the question we need to ask ourselves is whether we really need to print entire houses in the future …What reasons could there be? Let us fantasize!
The 90-degree angle will be forbidden by law as a relic of the industrial revolution, identified as one of the major causes for the waste we produced back then. Thus, Additive Manufacturing has, of course, become the leading technology. On the other hand, this pushes the way we use materials towards recycling friendliness. Next scenario: manual labor

has become so expensive that nobody is able to afford traditional building methods anymore, therefore machines are needed to produce our homes. In this case we can already see different ways of producing our homes: self-elevating casting systems, robots that build houses or machines that extrude entire sections will be able to build the required building stock more efficiently. It is obvious that there will be no laws that forbid certain ways of designing but we really have to think about the way we choose the tools we use to create the current and future demand.

3D printing is new and everyone is talking about it – a fact that causes a huge problem. The hype currently created by a less educated army of journalists, news agencies and blogs all around promises us that, in the future, we will be able to print anything we might ever need. New innovations that will change our world appear every day. However, if you look closely it is only the name that changes and, voila, a "new" 3D printing technology has been invented, doing something a bit different than its competitors, being a bit faster, cheaper, better … Do a search not only for "3D printing" but also for "the world's first 3D printed …" and you will see that you need to hurry – there is not much left to 3D print first … Excuse the critical and cynical metaphor.

In education, we have to teach the younger generations to tackle current problems and show them how to prepare themselves to find solutions we may not yet have discovered. The most common answer by our architectural students to the question of how a specific complicated detail will be produced: It will be 3D printed! Really? Is that the Holy Grail and the solution to all our problems or just a lack of knowledge and a failure of our education?

6 Self test for water durability
7 Combining printed parts and standard aluminum extrusion profiles to create a shelf

As part of our first semester of the Master Program we open Pandora's box and challenge our students to develop an innovative building component from sketch to working prototype on a 1:1 scale. The course is called Bucky Lab and as the name implies it is the credo of the innovator Buckminster Fuller that empowers the freedom of the students: whatever you can imagine, you can build. Often, it is the first time in their lives that they see a huge toolbox including old as well as new production technologies. Conventional power tools are placed next to laser cutters and 3D printers. It is amazing how fast the students are able to adapt themselves as well as their designs to the tools available to them. We discovered that the fact that the students have access to laser cutters at the faculty already during the Bachelor Program already changed their thought process. The tool that cuts flat sheets of paper, cardboard and wood up to a certain thickness becomes the tool of choice whenever something has to be cut. The students immediately see the benefits of this fast and cheap technology to save labor by gaining precision at the same time. For those who ignore the other technologies the workshop has to offer it is a long wait until it is their turn. Those students, on the other hand, who are curious to learn to operate other tools than those they already know are faster at producing their prototypes and may only use the laser cutter for very delicate or organic shapes that are harder to achieve using conventional tools. It is a learning process to choose the right tools for building their prototypes, but we also teach them which tools will be the most appropriate ones if their product needs to be produced in a larger batch size.

One of the most problematic issues is the right vocabulary we have to teach. Since modern software often uses the traditional "plot" or "print" command to start a 3D printing, laser cutting or CNC milling action, the process is often wrongly named. It is a common occurrence that we need to ask twice to really understand what students actually want to do when they tell us that they are going to laser print a model out of cardboard. Or when the CNC mill suddenly becomes a plywood 3D printer, because a small Danish architectural office calls their CNC mill a 3D printer so that they can be found easier online, fulfilling the hunger for the 3D printing hype. By the way, did we mention that we have 3D coffee printers all over our faculty? It is a machine that creates coffee with different flavors fully automatically out of a variety of raw materials and hot water just by pushing a button…

If your only tool is a drill, every solution will be a hole. We already see handwriting as a fading skill due to the fact that the use of smartphones, computers and inkjet or laser printers makes our life so much easier, not to forget the comfort of the delete button or the spellcheck function in MS Word we really do not want to miss. That's fine – easier for everyone to read and we are also able to reduce the amount of paper sent around the world by using email. But ask yourself honestly, doesn't a love letter say much more if it is written in ink on paper instead of an A4 printout in MS Word, Arial 10 point?

It is the awareness of a conscious choice of weapons that we are asking for. Of course, fully automated production lines are the standard if we are talking about mass production. It is machines that build our cars, in some cases true robots in the shape of these brightly colored arms we

directly associate with industrial robots, but often also in the shape of a conveyer belt where different steps of actions take place to produce a piece fully automated. Officially, that is still a robot. So it is no wonder that IKEA's Billy Bookcase is nearly entirely made by machines or robots, but – oh wonder! – IKEA does not advertise the Billy Bookcase by highlighting the robot production method; it is simply their best choice of tools to produce this particular piece of furniture for the lowest price and therefore with the best profit.
And we all know what handcrafted cars cost; what a pity that most of us will never be able to afford such a beauty, but on the other hand we are able to save energy with low emission cars that are built by robots.

While the use of robots or automated machines in industry is the only logical way to produce affordable products in large numbers we see the possibilities to break out of the masses by using digital production technologies. This is also described as Mass Customization and one of the key factors to argue why a CNC router, a robot or even a 3D printer has its advantages in comparison with the more traditional production technologies.

The example of the hearing aid device was already mentioned, but it easily shows the advantages of additive manufacturing. The inner ear of the patient is 3D scanned or filled with a putty that will be 3D scanned later. The device is then printed according to the dimension of the patient's ear's geometry; the electronic components can be easily embedded and a perfect fit for the customer achieved. The machine actually creating these shapes layer by layer can produce one piece next to a differently shaped one placed on the same build platform. It is the perfect process for this device and, with no ear being equal to another, a perfect solution.

Mass customization has been applied in the automotive industry for a long time, but it differs with regard to additive manufacturing. The producer offers the customer a huge variety of choices to create the perfect customized car. But the idea behind this is a system that allows combinations of mass produced components to be assembled according to the customer's wish, and in addition to color, accessories and the choice of motor a car already has a seat that can be moved back and forth to accommodate drivers of different sizes. While this example is commonly known by most of us, it is also applicable to our facades and windows. These consist of profiles and components that can be assembled in nearly any dimension and configuration as long as they are flat. The system already has solutions for non-rectangular shapes like hexagons, triangles and the like even though these demand larger efforts and are much more expensive.

So, back to the question of what should be printed and what not. In general, one major advantage of the digital additive production technologies is the fact that we are able to produce everything that would have been very difficult or even impossible to build with the common subtractive technologies. Often, we need to make products out of different parts which are then assembled to create the finished item. Now, we can conceive parts or geometries that include complex channels, chambers or shapes that allow us to enhance the performance of our building components. Back when we published the first version of Rapids we already envisioned components that use these advantages; we have shown facade

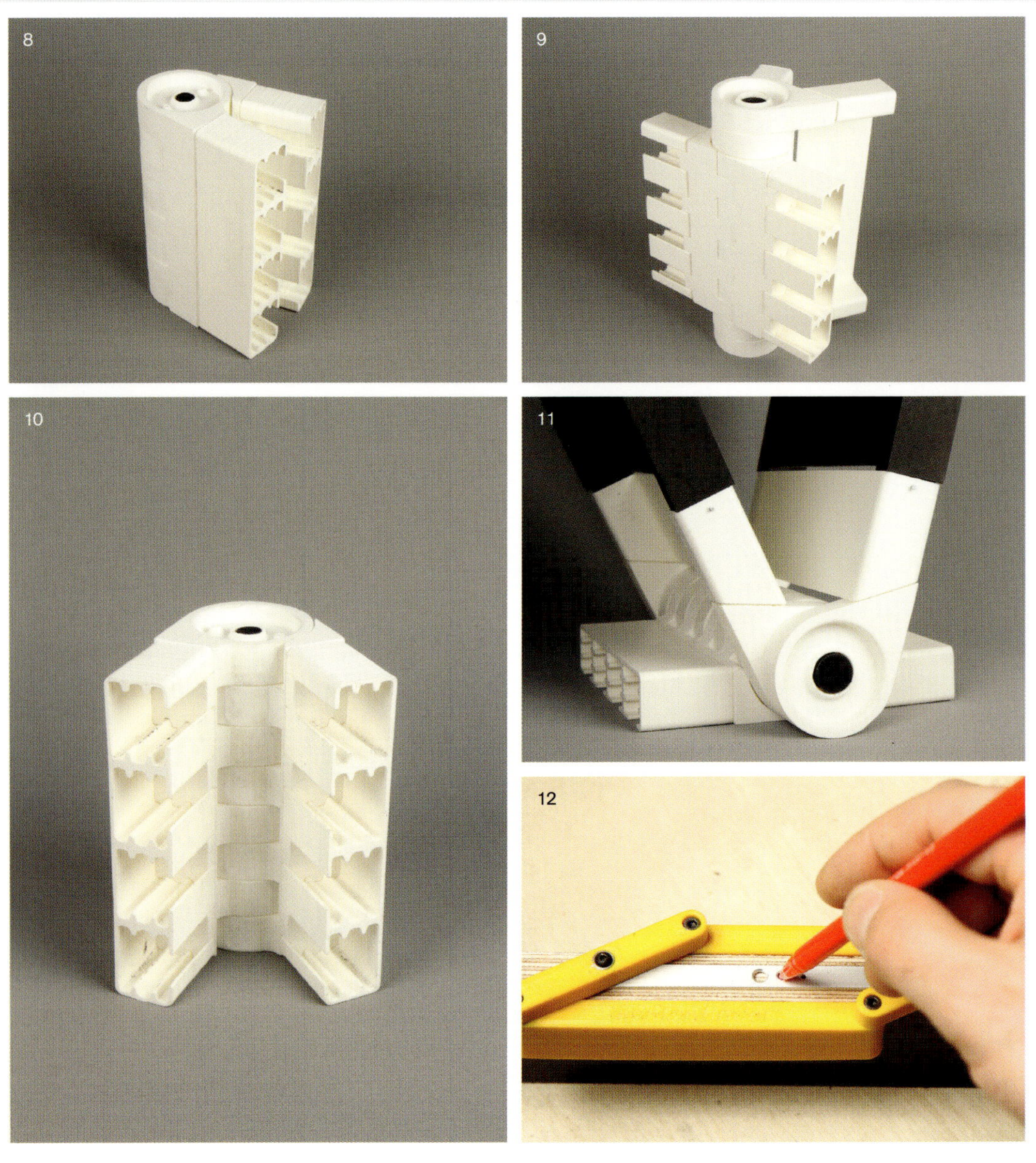

8-11 Using Additive Manufacturing to rapidly develop products. In this case a cast steel node for a foldable bridge (design: Elia Galiouna)

12 Using 3D printing you are able to produce custom made tools – here a centre finding tool based on a concept by Woodpeckers®

elements that follow the path of the forces, are shape-optimized to minimize the use of material and stiffer due to the fact that the parts are optimized for this special application. We have talked about internal tubes and channels that are able to serve as sun collectors or include heating systems.

In the automotive world we already see that happen in smaller sized parts, with cooling channels placed close to the contour that would have been impossible to fabricate with standard production technologies – even the best drill cannot drill curved holes. Imagine how compact an engine block would become if we were able to produce these parts with the least amount of material possible. But we also see that the machines that can print steel and other high performance materials are only slowly evolving due to the fact that the demand is still limited and the technologies are so expensive. Scaling up to house size will take time, and a decade seemed to be more realistic than just a few years.

But if we look towards the other arm of the digital production technologies using the more classic methods of subtractive manufacturing there is an obvious trend right now in the scale of our buildings. Using three or more axis CNC milling machines or the use of a robot with a router for more experimental purposes to construct buildings or building components shows that the feasible scale has broadened to encompass entire houses created from a digital file. Peter Stoutjesdijk, a former student at the Faculty of Architecture at TU Delft brought home the principles of friction fit connections from MIT's Larry Sass. In essence, this is a grown up version of the more basic WikiHouse principle. Using standard sized sheets of plywood, he is capable of creating wall, roof and floor elements that can be easily produced with his CNC mill. These parts can be easily assembled because they fit into each other like a big three-dimensional puzzle. The system can be optimized by nesting the parts with less than 5% of waste; due to the precision of the process and modern tool bits these parts and components can be joined airtight with the least amount of glue possible. Tolerances are only acceptable if they relate to the elongations of the material itself, but not to assembling or production errors. The first houses are already built, with more to follow. This technology offers the advantage of combining existing materials with machines that have been available for more than four decades without modification, but now for a new purpose.

3D printing for architectural purposes is actually a research and experimenting field in all disciplines; since it means using new machines and new materials for new purposes it is clear that we have to wait a bit longer to order our entirely printed house.

But what will we see in the closer future? It will be the combination of old and new. Imagine printed nodes that join standardized members like beams or struts, special fittings for installations that connect standard pipes, compact components that are able to save space due to a more compact inner geometry, free-form clay bricks that can form new geometries in direct combination with standard bricks.

Decide for yourself – it is up to you to create our future, but think about the purpose. We will only be able to successfully use these new technologies if we are able to add value to a product. Just because "we can" only works for the world's first…

4. AM SESSIONS

INTRODUCTION

Two think-tanks on Additive Manufacturing (AM) were hosted at the Universities of Technology in Delft and Darmstadt. The goal of these think-tanks was to address the possibilities, challenges and ongoing projects of AM in the built environment.
The two sessions were attended by different disciplines from the building industry. Architects and civil engineers discussed how AM could be implemented in the industry. The enthusiasm of speakers and audience resulted in a vital discussion that covered all aspects that need to be considered before AM can be used in our built environment. This chapter shows the lectures and topics addressed during those days based on the questions posed in the think-tank announcement.

AM is referred to as a very promising technology, but what are the important functions and characteristics of produced building components? Can additively manufactured elements already be implemented widely in the building industry, or should the performance be improved first?
The think-tank concept focuses on the implementation of AM in the building industry, trying to answer questions regarding durability, (anisotropic) material behavior and the kinds of materials that can be used. Can different materials be combined in an AM production process, or are "new" materials with matching production techniques desired? These are questions that will arise, but there are certainly even more challenging issues that will need to be addressed.

During the discussion we invited the audience and speakers to be creative and think about the application of AM, but (building) regulation was a topic as well. How does AM fit into the building industry's standards and legislation? We are not conceiving ideas for consumer products. The faith we have in our building industry and the quality and safety of buildings we are used to is something that should not suffer under a new production technology. So let us give the building industry a boost with Real Additive Manufacturing!

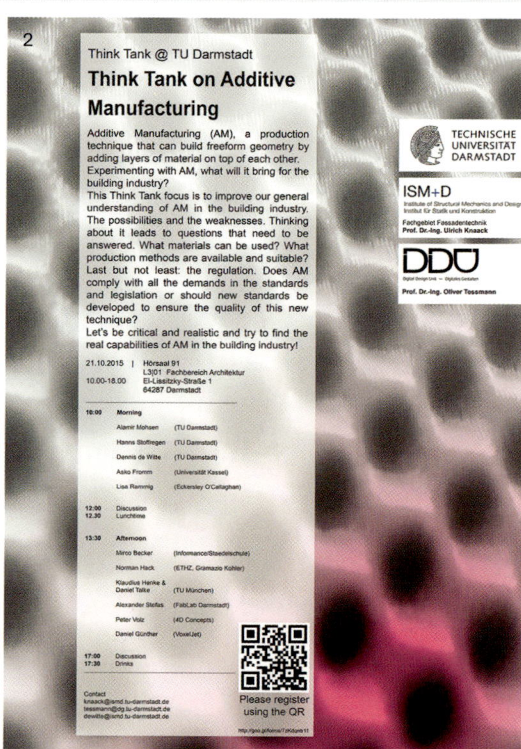

3-4 Real Additive Manufacturing TU Delft
5-6 Think-tank TU Darmstadt

MATERIAL PROPERTIES OF ADDITIVELY MANUFACTURED PARTS
MESH MOLD
OPTIMIZING STRUCTURAL BUILDING ELEMENTS IN METAL BY USING
  ADDITIVE MANUFACTURING
POTENTIAL OF LIGHTWEIGHT CONCRETE FOR ADDITIVE
  MANUFACTURING IN CONSTRUCTION
ROBOTIC BUILDING
3D CEMENT OBJECTS MADE USING INKJET PRINTING TECHNIQUES
3D PRINTED CASTING MOLDS – NEW OPPORTUNITIES FOR FORMWORK
3D PRINTING CONCRETE
3D PRINTING FOR SERIAL PRODUCTION – POSSIBILITIES AND
  LIMITATIONS

MATERIAL PROPERTIES OF ADDITIVELY MANUFACTURED PARTS

Wessel W. Wits, Faculty of Engineering Technology,
University of Twente

Additive Manufacturing (AM) produces parts essentially different from those made with conventional reductive techniques. Parts are usually constructed in a layer-by-layer fashion, whereby the geometric information of each layer comes directly from a digital (CAD) file that is sliced according to a predetermined build direction. Due to this way of manufacturing, the material properties of the part are on the one hand influenced by the properties of each fabricated layer and the way they interconnect, but on the other hand the build direction also leaves its mark on the overall part. Research has shown that a thorough understanding of both facets is critical in order to determine the material properties of additively manufactured parts.

The figures demonstrate examples of both effects. The images present a part with a tailor-designed internal fluid channel that allows fluid to pass effortlessly in one direction; however, in the opposing flow direction much more internal resistance is encountered. The fluid channel is tailored to a specific Reynolds number (a measurement for the flow characteristics). The shape of the internal structure can be seen in the X-ray observation. The effect of the build direction is also clearly visible as the internal structure is not as well rounded as it was designed. And, on the outside of the part the layered manufacturing method can be observed. Parts produced via AM will have a relatively high surface roughness as compared to parts made with conventional reductive techniques. Post-processing of an AM part is therefore common practice. This is shown in figure 5, in which two printed parts are joined using laser welding. The weld surface is smooth due to a post-process machining operation, whereas the other part surfaces were left untouched.

The part is produced from metal, in this case a Titanium alloy, using selective laser melting (SLM) as AM fabrication technique. Due to this process, a deviation from the original digital (CAD) part can be observed. For instance, the CAD comparison shows geometric deviations that can be attributed to the choice of build direction. As the part "grows" in the build direction the layers tend to sink in a bit. Although this is compensated for, small deviations between the designed and produced part may occur. Also, small voids (i.e. porosities) can be detected showing that small disturbances may occur during the fabrication of each layer. In general, these disturbances tend to show up near internal features and the part's external surfaces. Such disturbances are generally not an issue for the integrity of the part.

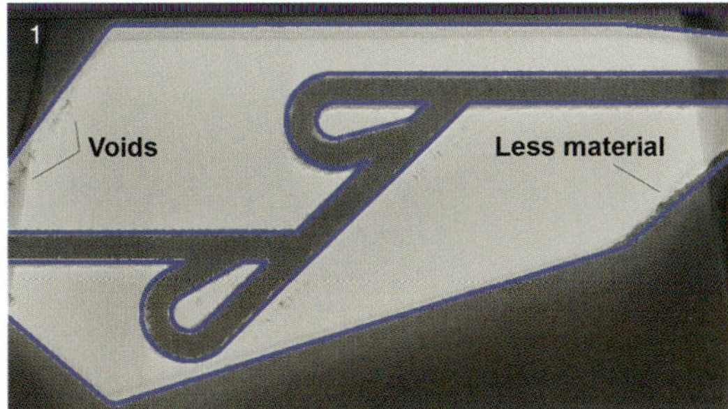

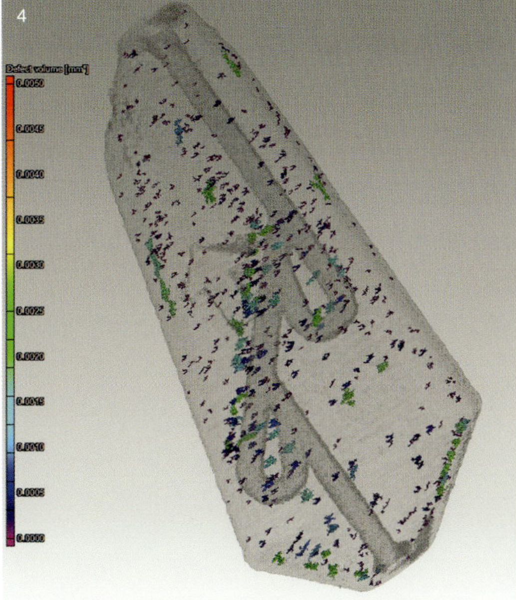

1 CAD to part comparison on an internal section of interest for Tesla valve structure; CAD outline is shown in blue. Image courtesy of University of Twente

2 Selective Laser Melted (SLM) part featuring a tailor-designed internal fluid channel. Image courtesy of University of Twente

3 2D X-ray observation of the internal fluid channel. Image courtesy of University of Twente

4 Void and porosity detection using 3D X-ray CT. Image courtesy of University of Padua in collaboration with University of Twente and NLR

5 Joining two SLM parts using pulsed laser welding after a post-processing operation. Image courtesy of University of Twente

MESH MOLD

Norman Hack

The research project Mesh Mold addresses the 1:1 construction aspects of robotically fabricated load-bearing structures. Considering the use of standard industrial robots with their limited payload capacities, however with a high capacity for precise spatial coordination, optimal use of the machine requires construction processes with minimal mass transfer and a high degree of geometric definition. Consequently, the fabrication of formwork for material-efficient and therefore geometrically complex concrete elements constitutes the focus of this investigation. Mesh Mold combines formwork and reinforcement into a single robotically fabricated construction system. The project (Patent Publication No. WO/2015/034438) was conducted in close collaboration with Sika Technology AG as an industry partner and expert in cementitious materials.

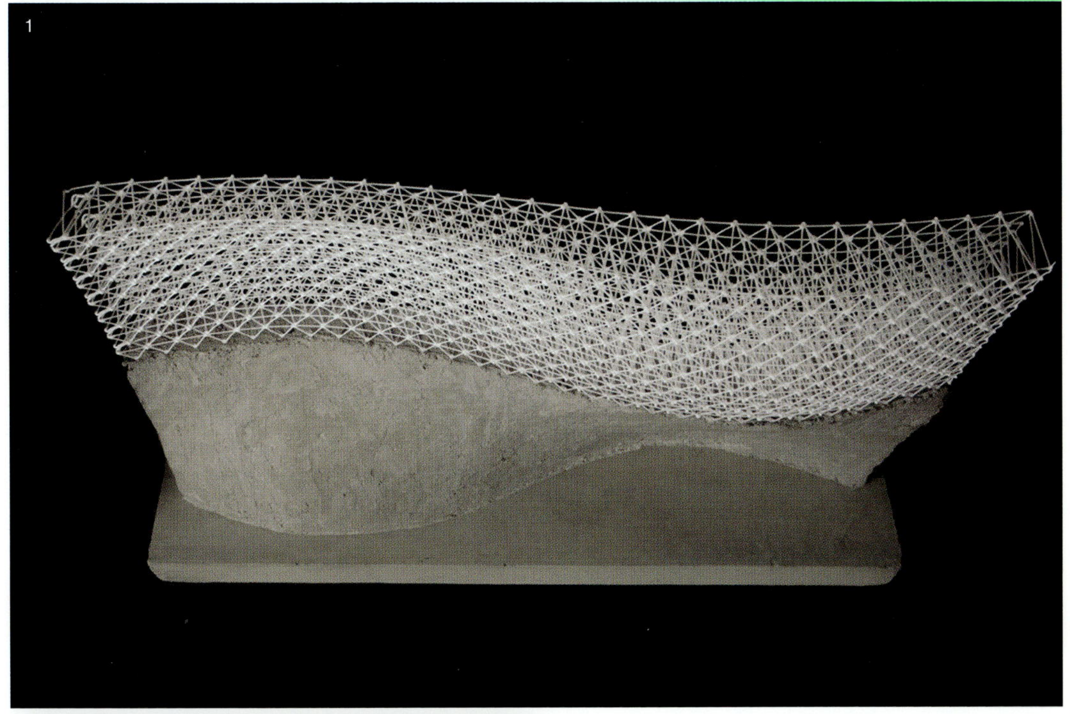

1 Mesh Mold exhibition concrete model. Image courtesy of Norman Hack Gramazio Kohler Research, ETHZ
2 Mesh Mold extrusion close-up. Image courtesy of Norman Hack Gramazio Kohler Research, ETHZ

OPTIMIZING STRUCTURAL BUILDING ELEMENTS IN METAL BY USING ADDITIVE MANUFACTURING

Salomé Galjaard, Sander Hofman, Shibo Ren, Neil Perry

By now everyone is used to the idea of 3D printing in metal and the fact that the technique allows for weight optimization, mass customization and product integration. What will be experienced however, while designing for this production technique, is the effect that even a few optimized elements can have on the total structure. In our case, we achieved a weight reduction of 75% per node, but when we analyzed the effect this had on the overall tensegrity structure that we were designing, we found out that tension and compression in the cables and struts was reduced by 20% because of it. This allowed us to replace all of these components with lighter versions, reducing the overall weight of the structure by almost 50%.

Originally, the structures were to be suspended from existing buildings that had to be reinforced accordingly. We expect that such reinforcement would not be necessary with the optimized (lighter) structure. This project taught us that you could bring your design to the next level of optimization when you consciously consider the role of an element as part of the bigger context.

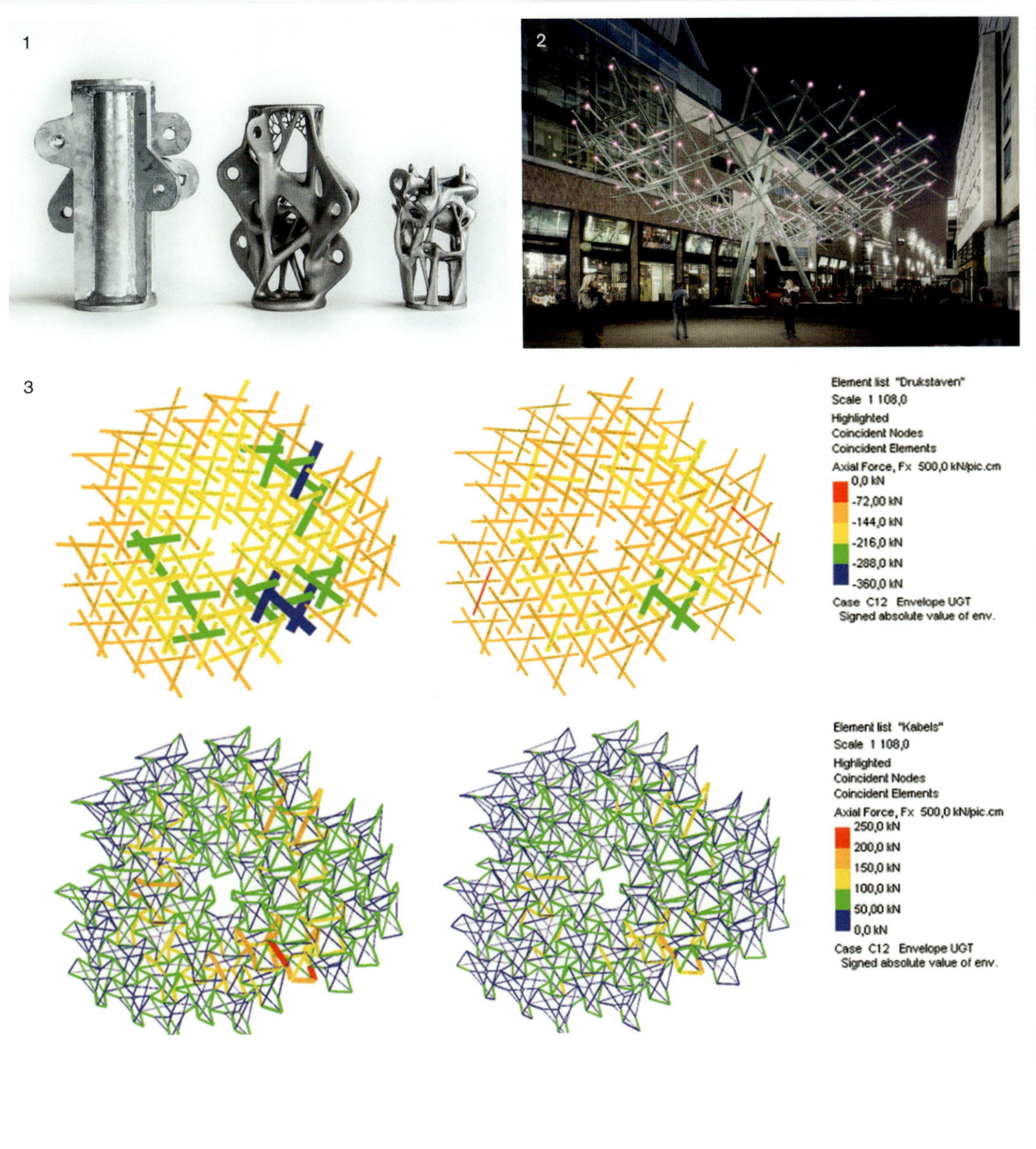

1 The three structural elements shown are all designed to carry the same structural loads and forces. The middle and right ones are produced by Additive Manufacturing. © Arup/Davidfotografie

2 Artist impression of one of the original tensegrity structures in The Hague. Architect: ELV Architecten © Studio i2

3 The forces in the struts (top) and cables (bottom) compared after weight adjustment of the nodes. © Arup

POTENTIAL OF LIGHTWEIGHT CONCRETE FOR ADDITIVE MANUFACTURING IN CONSTRUCTION

Klaudius Henke, Daniel Talke, TU München
Chair of Timber Structures and Building Construction

Its property of being freely shapeable in its fresh state to later solidify into a firm and durable artificial stone makes concrete appear to be a promising building material for Additive Manufacturing in building construction. However, the high firmness of the material goes along with high weight and thermal conductivity, leading to limitations related to manufacturing and transportation as well as the possible spectrum of application.

During Additive Manufacturing related work at the Chair of Timber Structures and Building Construction at TU München, the common heavy aggregates in the concrete are replaced with lightweight, mineral or plant-based aggregates. The resulting lightweight concrete shows lower firmness values, but it does allow for shape-optimized monolithic envelope elements without the need for additional thermal insulation. Geometric differentiation on the inside of the building part can achieve further optimization. Since overhangs can be realized to a certain extent, support structures can be realized as well. Lightweight concretes can be easily processed with subtractive methods, increasing geometric freedom and resolution at high building speeds.

1-3 3D printer, TU München
4 3D printed lightweight concrete. Image courtesy of Klaudius Henke
5 Subtractive finishing of 3D printed lightweight concrete part (sample fabricated by S. Stanglmayr).
   Image courtesy of Klaudius Henke

ROBOTIC BUILDING
CUSTOMIZED DESIGN TO ROBOTIC PRODUCTION FOR ADDITIVE MANUFACTURING

Henriette Bier, TU Delft

The Robotic Building (RB) project is based on the assumption that the factory of the future in building construction employs robotized processes that allow energy and material efficient building. Started in 2014 at Hyperbody, TU Delft, with a team consisting of assistant professor Henriette Bier, PhD candidate Sina Mostafavi, researchers Ana Anton and Serban Bodea and student assistant Marco Gali, the project aims to establish the Design to Robotic Production (D2RP) and operation framework allowing successful implementation of robotic production at building scale. The D2RP framework exploits expert and user involvement challenging the production/consumption gap by connecting parametric models with robotized production tools in order to achieve efficient production of custom-made parts for personalized use.

The RB project explores and advances D2RP by implementing experiments with MSc students. It builds upon knowledge in numerically controlled design to production processes developed during the last decade at Hyperbody, and profits from the support of 3TU, 100% Research, KUKA, ABB, and Delft Robotics Institute.

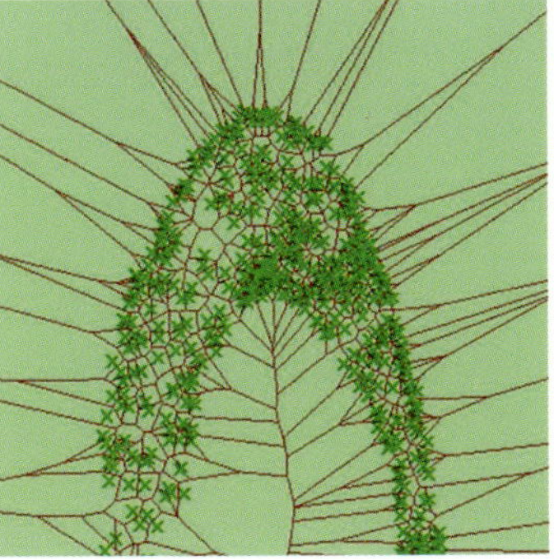
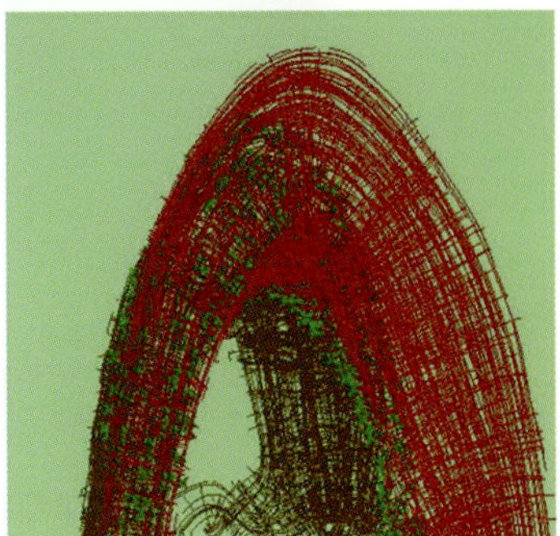

Customized Design to Robotic Production for Additive Manufacturing. Image courtesy of Henriette Bier, TU Delft

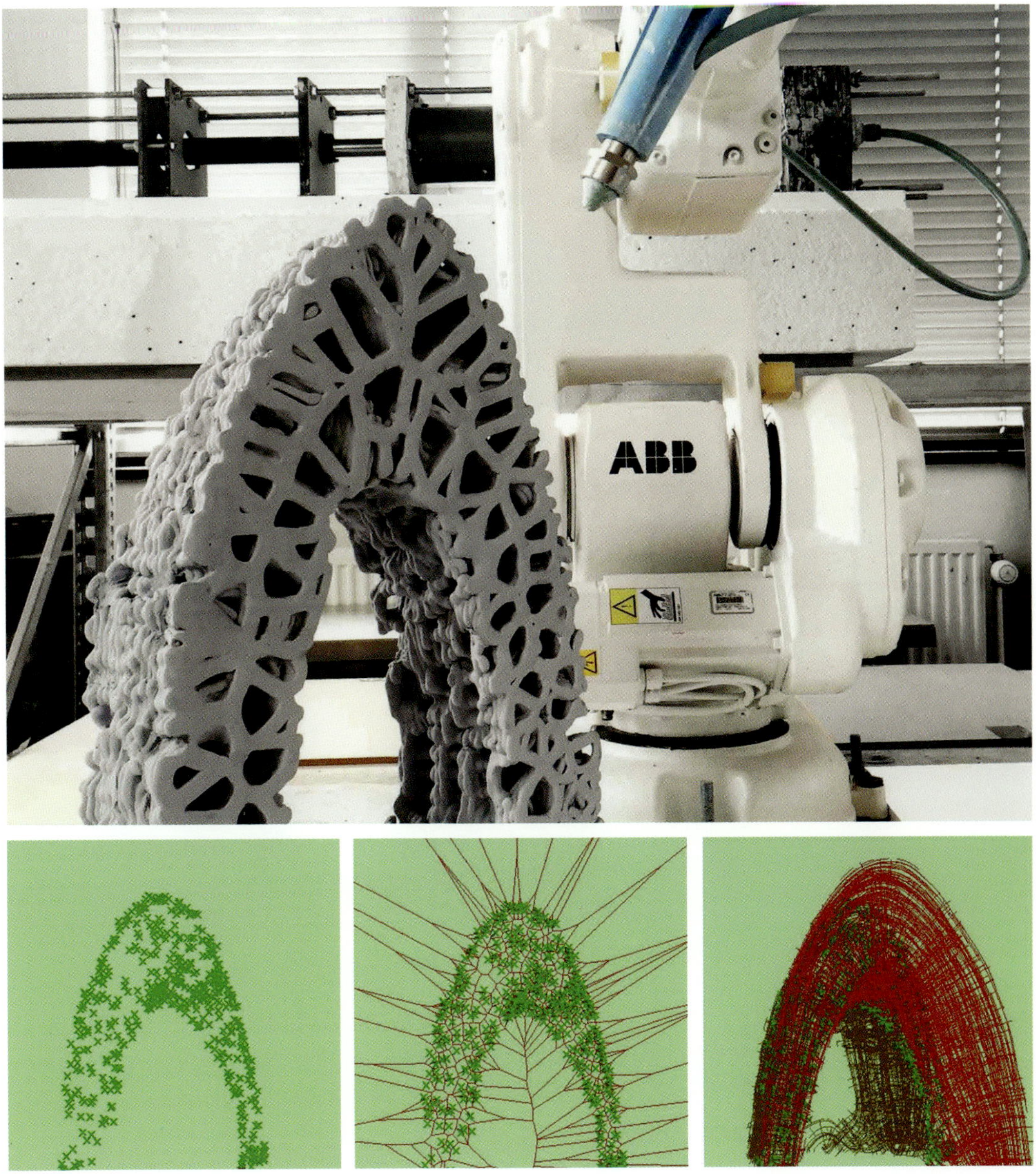

3D CEMENT OBJECTS MADE USING INKJET PRINTING TECHNIQUES

Asko Fromm

3D printing methods allow for the economical production of geometrically complex objects, even in small quantities. Therefore, the use of Additive Manufacturing methods has become standard in industrial product development.

Direct manufacturing of ready-to-use final products is becoming an established method for small parts such as jewelry, for example.

In architecture, with its need for large and geometrically complex building parts – often enough in small quantities – 3D printing technologies have remained largely unused. One of the materials well known in the field of architecture and interesting with regard to this manufacturing technology is the affordable material cement, not least due to its suitability for large parts.

Since 2008, Asko Fromm has researched the development and use of cement-bound products for architecture and the building industry, processed by means of the 3D printing method, as well as new forms of reinforcement that can be produced with these methods.

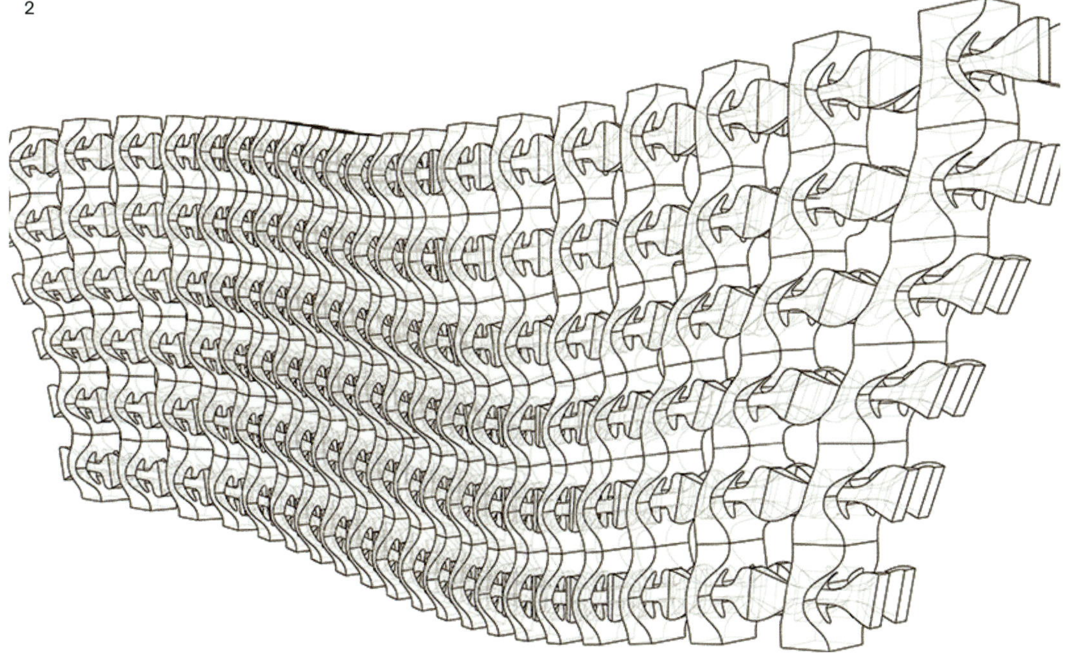

1 Additive manufactured concrete. Fromm, A. (2014), *3-D-Printing zementgebundener Formteile: Grundlagen, Entwicklung und Verwendung.* (Dr.-Ing.), Kassel: Kassel University Press, p. 117
2 Parametric model by Dr. Markus Schein

3D PRINTED CASTING MOLDS – NEW OPPORTUNITIES FOR FORMWORK

Florian Mögele, R&D, Voxeljet

3D printed casting molds are becoming increasingly important in industrial production. Even today, the casting industry often employs 3D printed casting molds, which have partially replaced conventionally produced molds. Small to medium sized series can be realized. Besides metal casting, the printed molds can be used for cold-hardening material systems such as concrete or artificial resins. Complicated geometries with undercuts, ornaments or inscriptions, very difficult or entirely unfeasible with conventional formwork, are easy to realize with 3D printed formwork.

1 3D printed formwork. Image courtesy of Voxeljet AG
2-3 Cast concrete. Image courtesy of Voxeljet AG

3D PRINTING CONCRETE

Gregor Zimmermann

Additive Manufacturing with 3D printed concrete enables the realization of complex geometries and objects for various applications that could not be realized with regular cast concrete. The pure cement-based and only water activated bonded material is highly ecological and economical. Resolutions of 300 μm and, with the latest optimized developments, of 100 μm allow the printing of highly detailed surfaces and objects. With a compressive strength of currently 5 Mpa and a weight of 2kg per liter, the printed material is as strong as common porous lightweight concretes. Optional additional coatings as well as post processing methods strengthen the surface resistance of the 3D printed elements.

Next to applications in architecture, such as statues or reliefs in the field of old-building renovations, the use in aluminum casting allows mind-blowing possibilities compared to common sand core prints. An up to 1200°C heat resistant 3D printed concrete mold can be reused several times, depending on its geometry. Porosity allows gases from the hot aluminum to evacuate, thus generating nearly perfect aluminum surfaces that usually do not require post-processing.

The material offers another sustainability advantage – powder not used during the print can be used in the following printing batch. The printing process and thus the parts do not contain any toxic or waste materials at all.

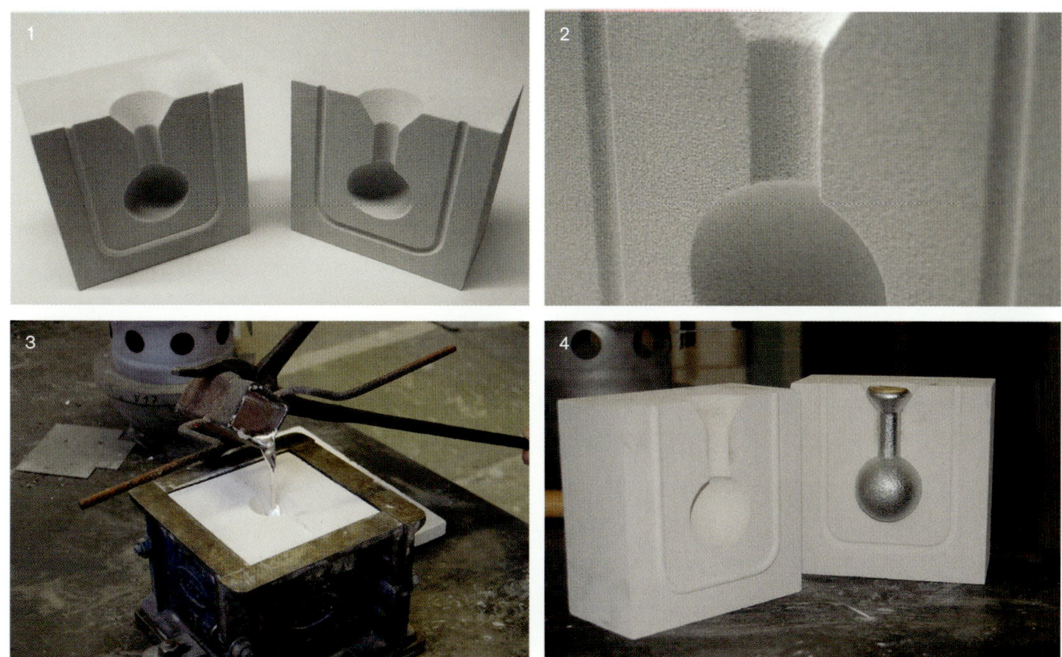

1 3D printed aluminum mold. Image courtesy of Gtecz
2 3D printed aluminum mold, close-up. Image courtesy of Gtecz
3 Casting 3D printed aluminum mold. Image courtesy of Gtecz
4 Cast 3D printed aluminum mold. Image courtesy of Gtecz

3D PRINTING FOR SERIAL PRODUCTION – POSSIBILITIES AND LIMITATIONS

Peter Volz, 4D Concepts GmbH

3D printing – in the early stages known as and used for Rapid Prototyping – has become a general term for all Additive Manufacturing processes. However, this technological field encompasses a diverse range of processes with sometimes fundamental differences. Besides 3D printing systems to create models for shape-finding and communication during the product development phase, there are Rapid Manufacturing systems for Additive Manufacturing of technically complex prototypes up to small series production. These methods have been used in industrial manufacturing for more than 25 years, but technical limitation restricts their spectrum of application here as well.

The processes will find their way into the building industry and architecture. Fast and safe communication with printed models supports architects and planners even now. However, standard production of entire buildings does not seem feasible in the foreseeable future, but 3D printing can indeed be the solution in this area when considering specific aspects, e.g. structural building parts and facade elements.

1-2 Architectural model of Dresden. Image courtesy of 4D Concepts
3 Sintered part of Spaceport. Image courtesy of 4D Concepts

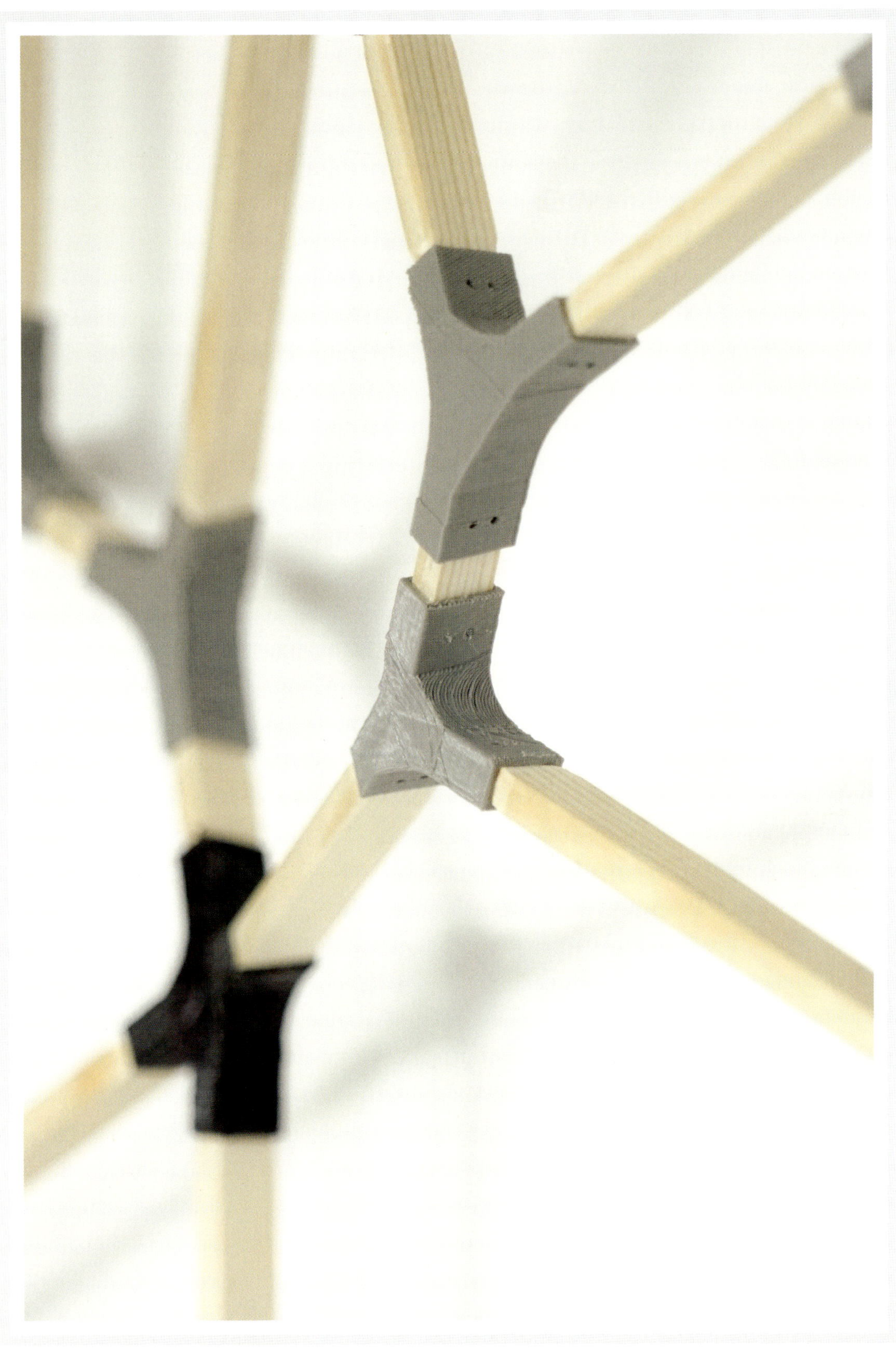

5. AM PROJECTS

ADDITIVE MANUFACTURING FOR DAYLIGHT
AM OF GLASS
AM ENVELOPE
BIM FOR AM ENVELOPES
CERAMICS IN AN AM PROCESS FOR THE BUILDING INDUSTRY
CONCRETE IN AN AM PROCESS
CONVECTIVE CONCRETE
FREEFORM CONCRETE PRINTING: A HYBRID SYSTEM FOR
FABRICATING COMPLEX CONCRETE GEOMETRIES
HYBRID BUILDING CONSTRUCTION
INTERACTIVE STRUCTURES
THE "SOFT" SPONGY SKIN
THE SPONGY SKIN
VORONOI FACADE
1ST GENERATION PARAMETRIC NODE N-AM 01 TO 08
2ND GENERATION PARAMETRIC NODE N-AM 10
3D PRINTED FORMWORK FOR FREE-FORM CONSTRUCTIONS
20,000 BLOCKS ABOVE THE GROUND

ADDITIVE MANUFACTURING FOR DAYLIGHT

26-06-2015

IMAGINED BY Lemonia Karagianni
KEYWORDS printing, customization, product design, parametric design, daylight performance

Daylight control is one of the facade functions that affect user comfort. Different climates, functions and user preferences have a great impact on the design of sunshades, thus requiring customized solutions. Additive Manufacturing methods can produce customized objects with highly complex geometries. The main objective of this project is to explore the potential of Additive Manufacturing in the building sector by introducing non-standardized solutions for daylight and shading which can be customized by individuals according to their needs.

The parametric modeling tool is proposed because it can generate various designs based on different variables, while providing information about building performance as a result of design parameter updates. The performance of the sunshade is regulated by its geometry and the final product is fabricated by means of Additive Manufacturing. Therefore, an explicit association between geometry, fabrication and light control performance is suggested.

3D printed models, PET-PLA material

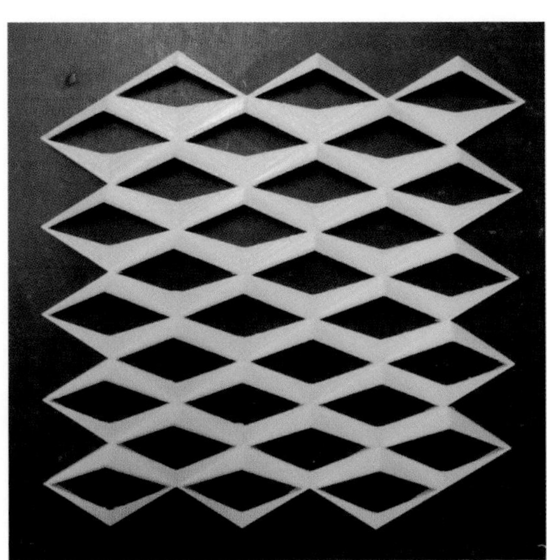

The concept introduces an interface, where users can choose and modify one of the specific geometries available in the online library of designs according to their own individual situation. The final product is an external 3D printed sunshade for window frames, produced directly from the computer file to the 3D printer (factory) and assembled with snap-fit connections.

1 Assembling of modules. Snap-fit joint.
  Male and female snap-fit connection
2 Example of design variations from user input
3 Interior view of proposed facade
4 User scenario

AM OF GLASS
05-05-2016

IMAGINED BY Lisa Rammig
KEYWORDS Additive Manufacturing, glass, welding, heat bonding

Glass has always fascinated the creators of buildings due to its very inherent property, its transparency. In Gothic cathedrals the transparency of the often colored glass was used to create mystical spaces. And still today, the transparency of the envelope is a major design component for architects and designers of buildings and interior spaces.

The transparency of the material makes the connections of a glass structure or facade even more important, as they define the appearance to a large extent. However, to provide structural integrity, commonly solid materials are required to connect the glass, resulting in non-transparent connections.

And even though over the past century glass has increasingly been used as a structural component, its inherent brittleness still requires solid connections to transfer loads.

During the past decades a vast development in structural glass envelopes and enclosures could be observed, aiming to achieve a maximum amount of transparency.

The development from an infill material to a structural material enabled designers to develop buildings that are based on using a large quantity of glass, i.e. atriums, skylights and structural glass enclosures.

These glass structures feature the ability to merge with their surroundings and become invisible, nearly dematerialized if the connections are kept to a minimum. This requires a large amount of structural engineering, detailed analysis and

Structural glass connection during heat bonding (welding) process

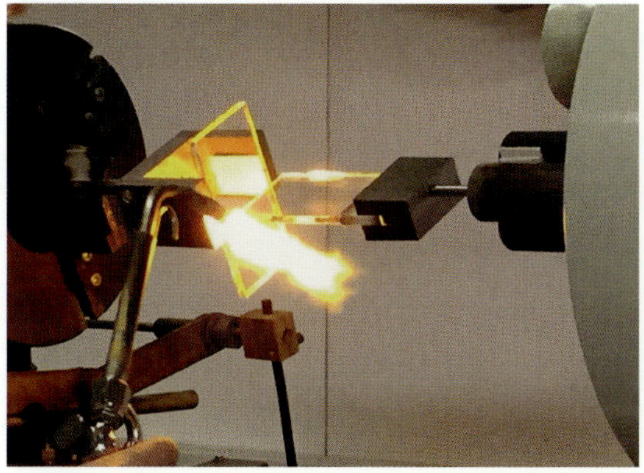
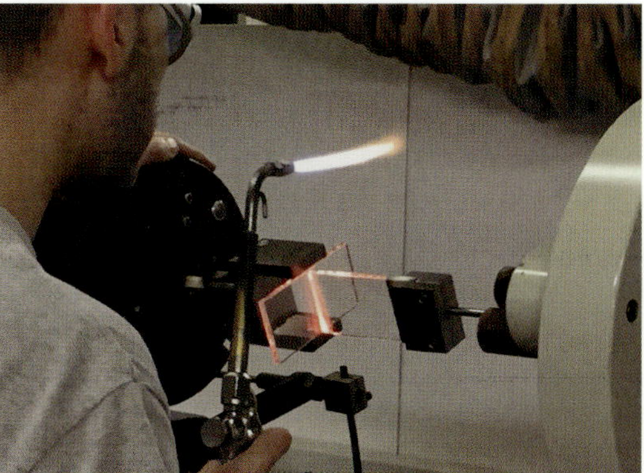

precise detailing to achieve sufficiently safe structures. Although a significant amount of research into transparent bonding materials and bonded connections has been undertaken in recent years, solid metal connections are still commonly used to form structural glass connections.

Thus, with the developments that can be observed in structural glass – tending to an optimization of connections and production capabilities and leading to a reduction of the number of fittings and an increase in transparency – further research is still required to innovate in this respect as opposed to improve existing technology to eliminate the necessity of opaque connections.

Based on the demand for transparency in glass structures and the desire by architects and designers to create fully transparent glass enclosures, this PhD research seeks to understand the opportunities and limitations of heat bonded, fully transparent glass connections without the use of an additional fixing material. Further to that, the impact of such connections on the transparency of an envelope is studied to understand the impact glass fixings have on the perception of transparency of a glass facade.

One experimental proposal is the heat bonding (welding) of borosilicate components to achieve mono-material transparent connections. Borosilicate is chosen in this case due to its low coefficient of linear thermal expansion (3.3 for Borofloat 33, 8.4 for soda lime silica).

To achieve atomic bonds, borosilicate glass is joined in a manual bonding (welding) process as a first step to understand the structural properties of the connections themselves.

Borosilicate glass is primarily used in the chemical and pharmaceutical industry due to its high chemical resistance and low coefficient of linear thermal expansion, which is essential when substances are to be heated in test tubes. Thermal tempering of borosilicate is extensively more sophisticated than the thermal tempering of soda lime. However, by rapid quenching and a decrease in the quenching temperature, Schott have developed a process to overcome problems caused by the low thermal expansion and can produce thermally tempered borosilicate.

In a preliminary study, several types of connections were manufactured to compare and evaluate atomic bonding. Firstly, the behavior of glass-glass connections was tested, as was the degree of precision with which they could be made. The applications of layer-by-layer fabricating were then completed to simulate a "real" additive process.
The testing of the welded connections suggested that failure of the material in most cases occurs within the region of the original material, confirming that the connections would be at least as strong as the parent material. This verifies that it is possible to manufacture glass with the additive processes to generate strong connections.

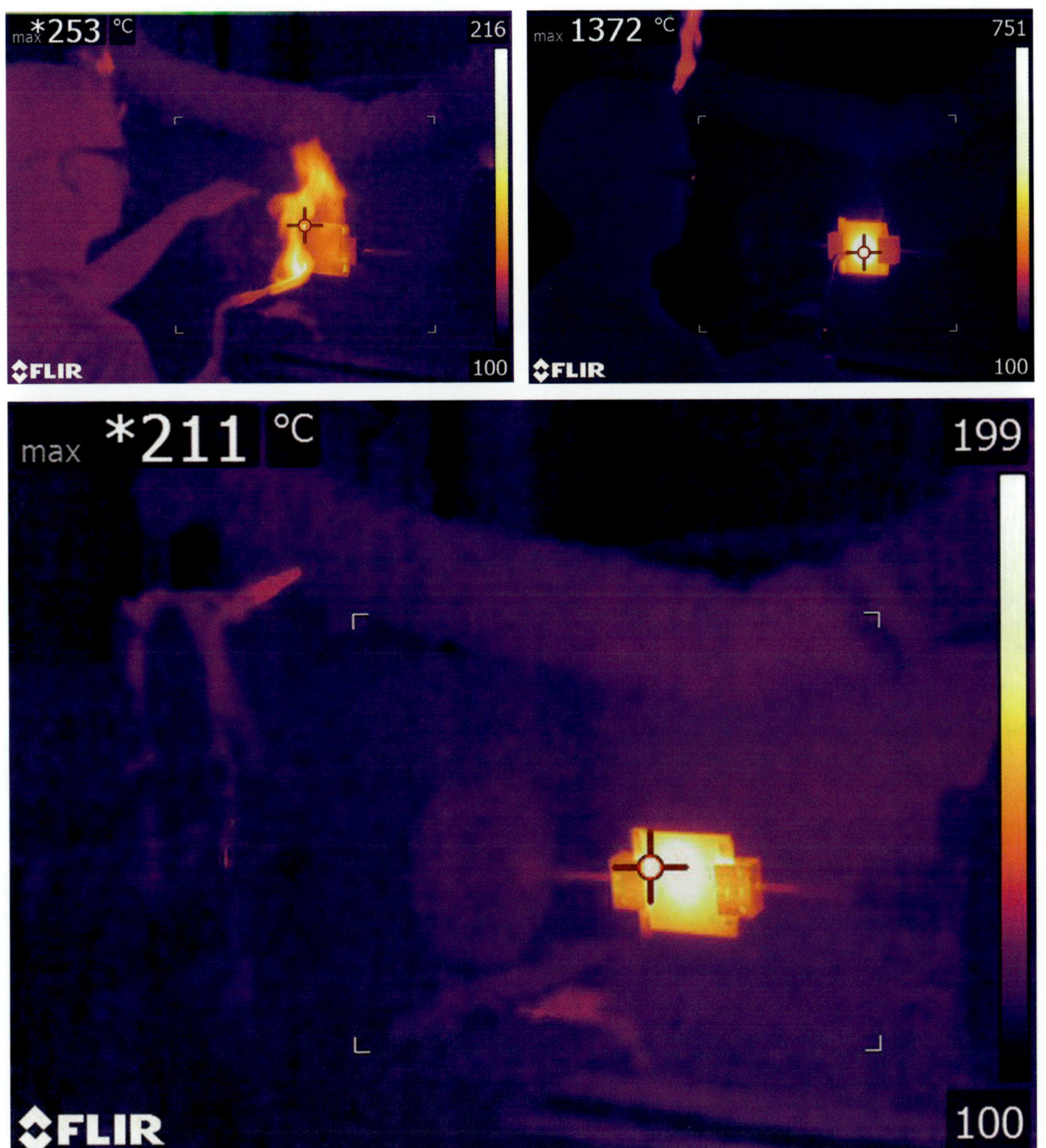

Temperature monitoring during welding process

AM ENVELOPE
14-01-2014

IMAGINED BY Holger Strauß
KEYWORDS new building materials, new material combination, smart facade components, change of ideals, AM envelopes

Additive Manufacturing (AM) for building envelopes has great potential: AM will change the way of designing facades, how we engineer and produce them, from a mere space enclosure to a dynamic building envelope.
It is a tool that is able to close another link in the 'file-to-factory chain'. AM allows us a better, more precise and safer realization of today's predominantly digital designs that are based on the algorithms of the available software. AM will never replace established production processes but rather complement them where this seems practical: towards hybrid building construction, the combination of human skill and craftsmanship with high-tech tools to translate the designers' visions into reality. This is pushing the boundaries of one's own trade or field of expertise (the aluminum working industry offers enhanced material components, e.g. ceramics or high-tech plastic components).

Nematox II

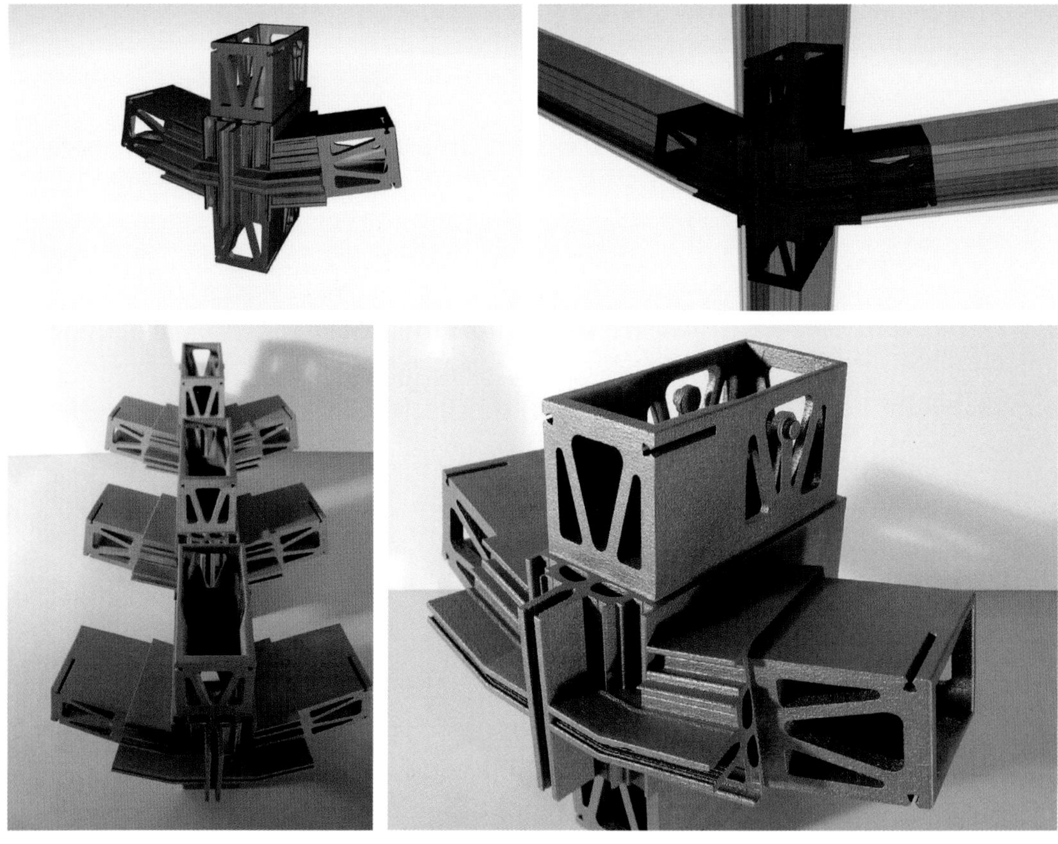

BIM FOR AM ENVELOPES
14-01-2014

IMAGINED BY Holger Strauß
KEYWORDS building process optimization, BIM, parametric design, digitally informed building construction

Observing the latest developments in the building construction process, Additive Manufacturing (AM) is at hand to accompany BIM and digital tools, applied to plan and construct today's buildings.
AM allows for parametrically controlled complex parts with varying geometries of continuous certification and quality. Parametric design allows for design within material boundaries (e.g.: only feasible set-ups supported by CAD-CAM centers).

BIM offers the chance to manage all aspects of informed building construction and combine well-known applications in an innovative way.

Relevant parameters:
- liability;
- simplexity;
- geometry;
- availability;
- uniqueness (one-off parts);
- cost and savings;
- structural integrity;
- material properties;
- etc.

1

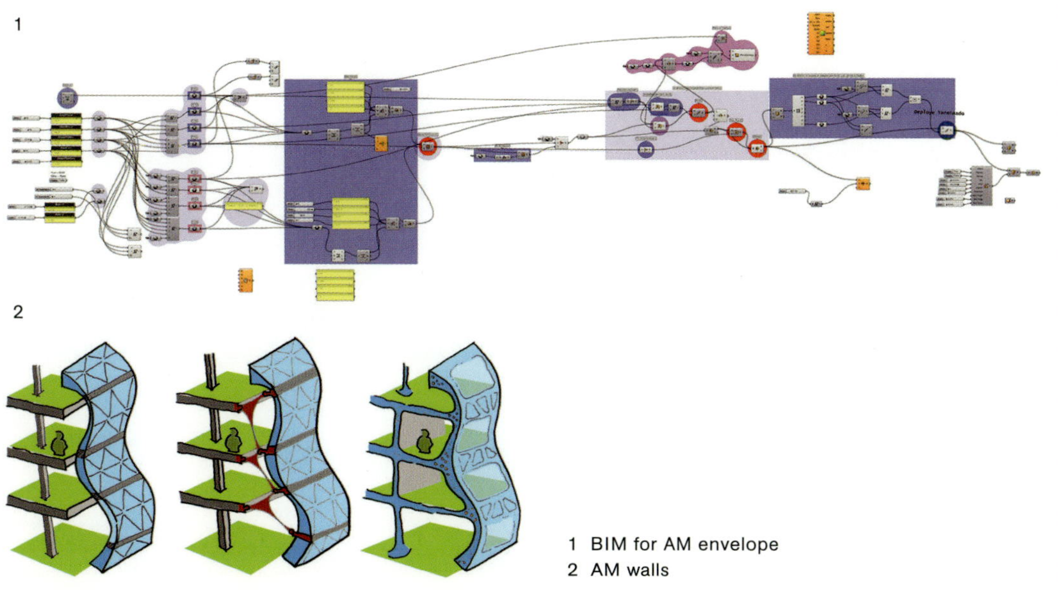

2

1 BIM for AM envelope
2 AM walls

CERAMICS IN AN AM PROCESS FOR THE BUILDING INDUSTRY

01-03-2016

IMAGINED BY Dennis de Witte
KEYWORDS clayey ceramics, Additive Manufacturing, integration, free-form, brick

Clayey ceramics are, next to steel, aluminum, wood, glass and composites like concrete, materials used in the construction industry. Until now, additive technologies in combination with ceramics have been used to create art and laboratory equipment. In order to use this technology for a variety of applications besides consumer products, the structural properties need to be known. The research project performed at TU Darmstadt focuses on the purpose for which Additive Manufacturing (AM) of clayey ceramics can be embedded in the built environment. The material characteristics and structural performance of those materials are part of the scope required to answer the research questions on how structural ceramic components perform within the built environment if produced with an Additive Manufacturing process to integrate functions and optimization in form, in order to increase the products' functionality.

Since AM is a layered production technology, most of the materials used have anisotropic properties. This has to do with the AM process and the print resolution used. With most materials, the hardening process into the final shape takes place during the shaping. A chemical reaction or melting and solidifying are examples of

Free form brick

Surface pattern brick

that. By contrast, for clayey ceramics the hardening of the shaped green bodies takes place during firing, where it vitrifies during the so-called glassification. This binds all of the material together simultaneously, and allows the compound to become an isotropic material. Compare the steps of the different materials in the production process scheme. The scheme shows how clayey ceramics are used in an AM process in comparison with other construction materials.

The main reasons for using AM are freedom of form, integrated functions that could not be embedded otherwise, and cost effectiveness for small batch sizes since formwork is not needed. To show the benefits of AM, three small brick projects were printed using Fused Deposition Modeling (FDM):

- Free-form
- Surface pattern
- Integrated mono-material products

To test the characteristics, standardized bricks were printed to be compared with normal clinker bricks.

FREE-FORM
Consider ceramic as a material for structural building components. Until now, production technologies were not adapted for free-form and small batch size building components, but that can change. If formwork or expensive dies for extrusion are no longer needed, the batch size will not influence the production costs anymore. Special corner bricks or even entire free-form walls for special projects can be additively manufactured.

Integrated mono-material products   Performance 3D printed bricks

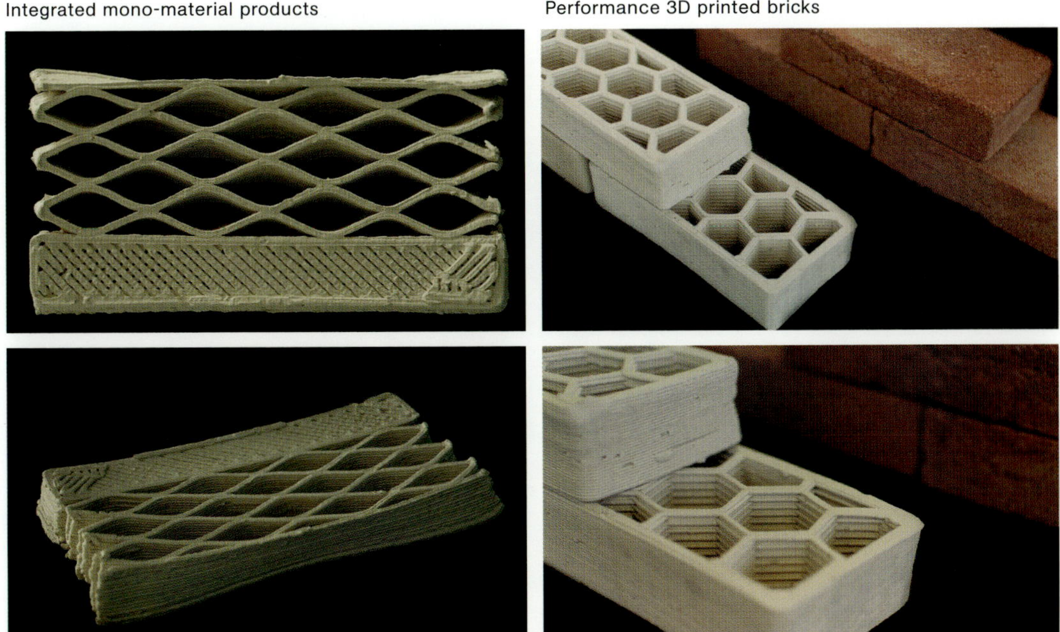

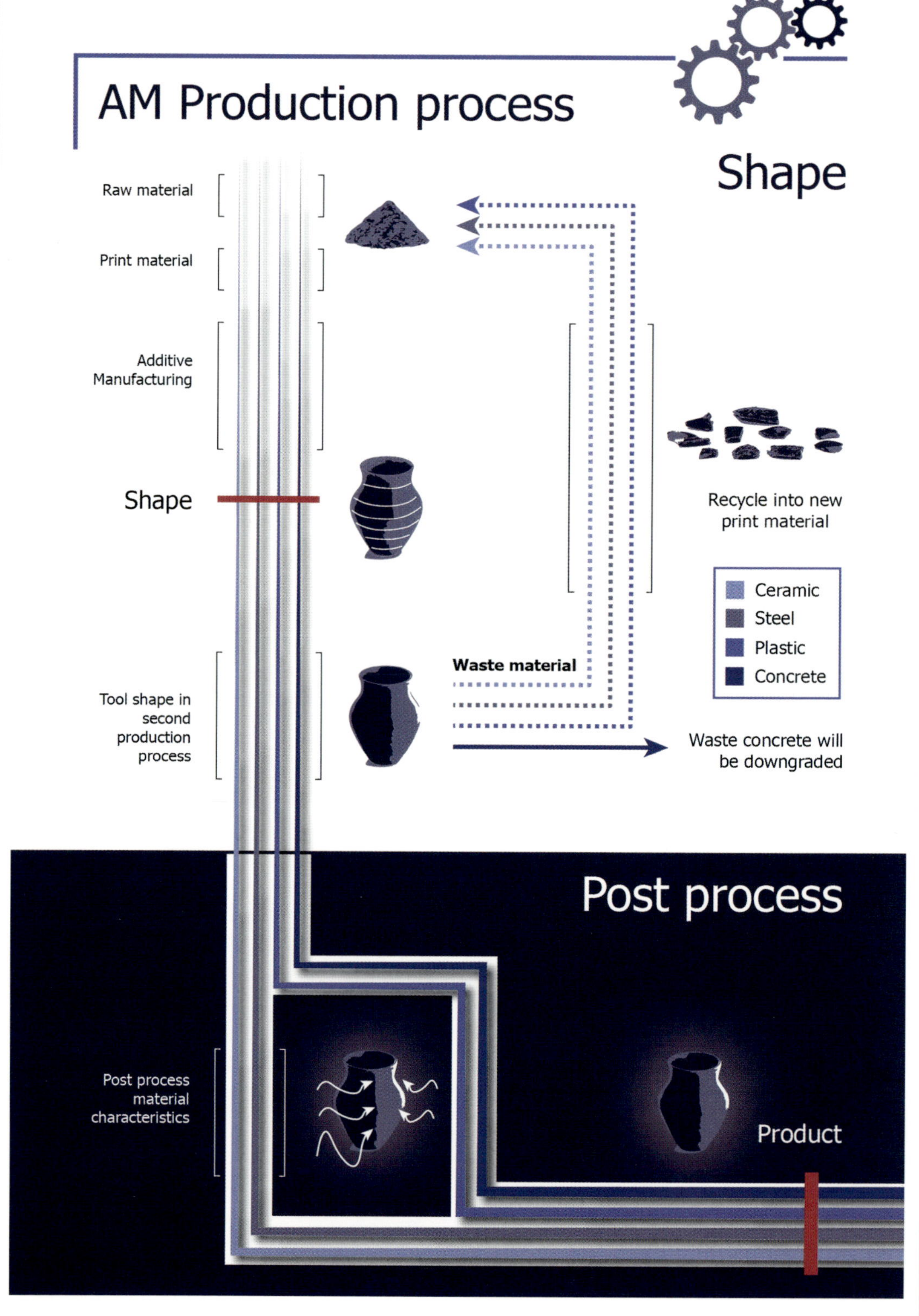

AM production process

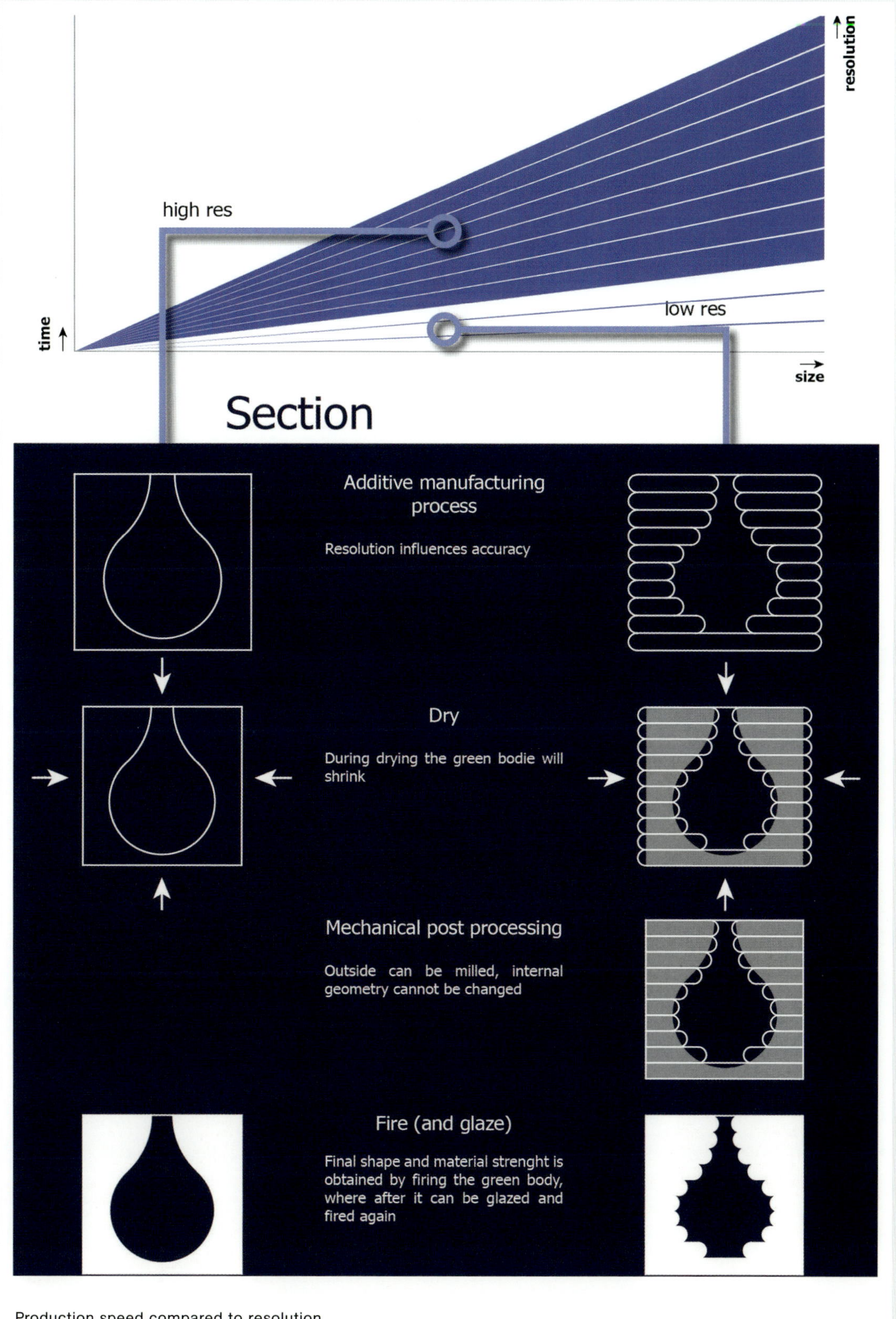

Production speed compared to resolution

SURFACE PATTERN

The produced bricks have a pattern that is difficult to produce with a mold or extrusion process. This particular surface pattern brick was printed using a continuous flow. The advantage of a continuous extrusion path, controlled by g-code, is that the filament is not interrupted, which allows a faster print process.

INTEGRATED MONO-MATERIAL PRODUCTS

A first example of a function integrated multi-layered element has been printed. The inner side will be the load-bearing structure, protected by a thin walled pattern as insulation, which is covered by an outside cladding. Such facade elements can be made using an extrusion process; however, this is impossible when complete freedom of form is desired.

This is yet another field where an AM process can be used as a production method for a mono-material construction with multi-functional performance. The ability to produce these combined elements out of one material is promising: there is an increasing demand for the raw materials to be recycled, but recycling components made out of different materials is difficult. Complete facades can be recycled easily when using one material to produce elements with voids that interlock mechanically.

Research on how 3D printed materials perform compared to traditionally produced products is conducted to get a general understanding of material behavior. Standardized stones have been printed for this purpose. Although it does not make use of the benefits of AM, it is a good way to compare the product's characteristics.

The 3D printed stones have different amounts of infill so as to also understand the influence of material interlocking during the compression tests. As described above, the main purpose is to obtain information about the structural characteristics to gather the knowledge needed to design new products for the facade industry. A look at deposition speed and resolution of the processes shows us that different resolutions for different products might be desired. The diagram of production speed versus resolution shows how the resolution influences the final geometry. Even with post processing, the resolution is still visible because the internal geometry is difficult to post process. Even when combining technologies to identify an economical alternative for slow AM processes, complex geometries cannot always benefit from combining additive and subtractive manufacturing.

Material samples of available technologies are compared to obtain the production characteristics of all of the different production technologies and material mixtures. These tests on structural performance and material characteristics compared with known material characteristics and performance give an understanding of the influence of AM on the processing of ceramic materials, and how additive manufacturing of ceramic structural components can be employed in the built environment.

CONCRETE IN AN AM PROCESS
30-01-2015

IMAGINED BY Dennis de Witte
KEYWORDS Additive Manufacturing, 3DP, FDM, concrete, match material and process, future vision, roadmap

Additive Manufacturing (AM) of concrete is a challenging field. The material and the manner of processing are just a first stage. Considering that the biggest benefit of concrete is its price, the prevailing approach to the AM of concrete, which consists of producing relatively low strength elements with a lot of expensive cement, is ineffective. To improve this, the material and the processing need to be integrated. Concrete differs in many ways from the materials that are commonly used in AM processes due to the chemical reaction involved.

The possibilities for products made with an additive process are endless, but to improve existing production methods with the use of additive ones does not mean that more freedom in form is the greatest improvement. The implementation of functions in traditional products can be even more valuable. An example is the integration of insulation in the core of cast walls, using AM to extrude these porous cores in between the watertight and load-bearing slabs. Free-form elements can also be made using an advanced molding technique. Internal gradient properties cannot be created otherwise. Added value is the aim that should be pursued in an AM process. AM has a great potential for the concrete industry, but in some cases the application is less visible, since implementation of functions is not always as prominent as free-form geometry.

The way concrete is processed by initiatives such as Contour Crafting or 3D Concrete Printing imposes on concrete a production technique that resembles Fused Deposit Melting (FDM). D-Shape, just like 3D Printing (3DP) uses a binding agent. All of those methods do not use concrete as described in the literature, but rather as a substitute for normal concrete in order to sell it. The material and the

Concrete in an AM-process roadmap (de Witte, 2015). Image can be downloaded from TU Delft repository.

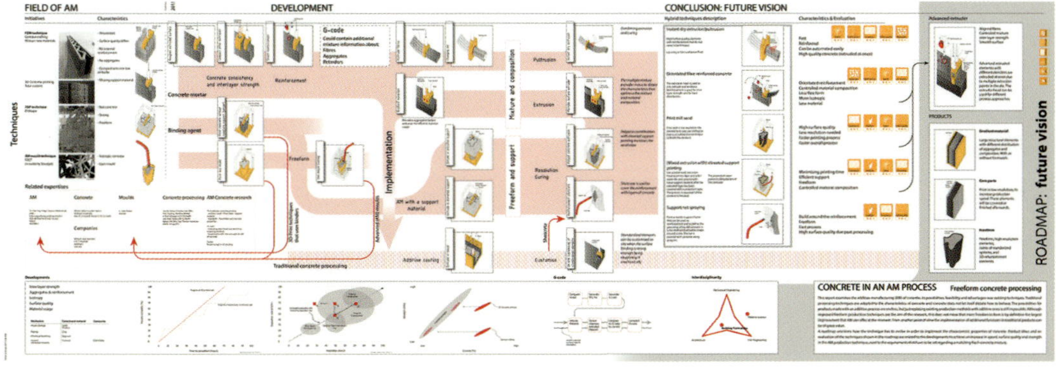

process should be changed to get the best results, but as far as information is available this has not been done yet. The findings of this research indicate that to get the best results the materials and processes used in present AM methods need to be changed and more aligned.

While exploring the above, it became clear that the main challenge of the AM of concrete is how the technique is used and the way the concrete is processed. The roadmap shows a summary of the existing processes and how they should evolve. The overall strength, inter-layer strength, reinforcement and the material composition are aspects that need to be developed first. The future vision showed five techniques that respect the characteristics of concrete, and issues regarding the evolvement of the technique are addressed within these visions. The challenge of how to implement the technique in the building process is harder to tackle, because a well-functioning technique as a free-form concrete processing principle does not exist yet. Since it is premature to talk about specific characteristics of the elements and whether AM should take place at the building site or not, a shift in the research focus toward processes has to be made. Nonetheless, it can be assumed with certainty that the production technique will develop in two directions in the near future – one towards large elements that can only be produced on site and the other towards high resolution elements that need to be made in a controlled environment for the best results.

Nevertheless, the requirements of the products are important in order to evolve the production technique and to examine the designed production process. Attention needs to be paid to the selection of the appropriate and adequate AM technique for a specific project.

Instant curing with a changing die

Interlayer strength with different concrete mixtures

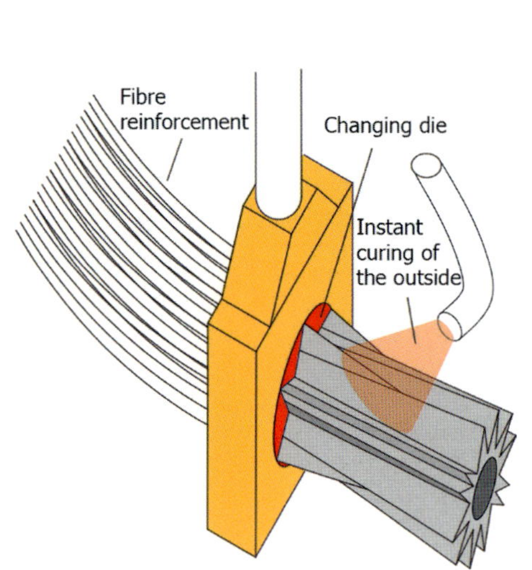

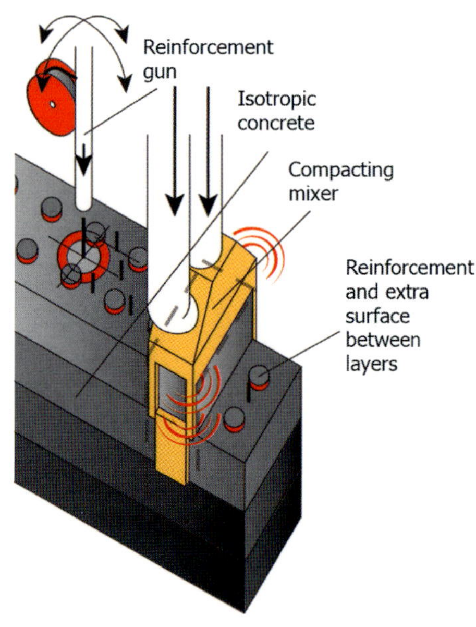

CONVECTIVE CONCRETE
01-03-2016

IMAGINED BY Dennis de Witte, Marcel Bilow, Roel van Loonen, Marie de Klijn
Ulrich Knaack, Jan Hensen
KEYWORDS advanced formwork, concrete, optimization, heat exchange,
heat storage

The social impact of this proposal concerns the 2020 goals focusing on
a reduction of emissions and an increase in thermal comfort within the
built environment.

Although thermal heat storage in concrete can fulfill a major role in the short
day-night temperature cycles to flatten the peaks, it is hard to thermally activate
the concrete's core during those short time intervals.

We pursue on-demand access to the buffered thermal energy in the complete
concrete element by increasing the speed and overall control of the charge/
discharge process.

With convective concrete, our dependency on heating, ventilation and air-
conditioning systems will decrease, while the convection within the concrete will
contribute to a higher thermal comfort and an increased rate of carbonation.
Through convection in the concrete core, the thermal storage performance can
be enhanced and better controlled and as such, make buildings more responsive
in a smart grid context. If the results are promising, standardized and one-off
solution elements can be embedded in our built environment within a few years.

Convective concrete

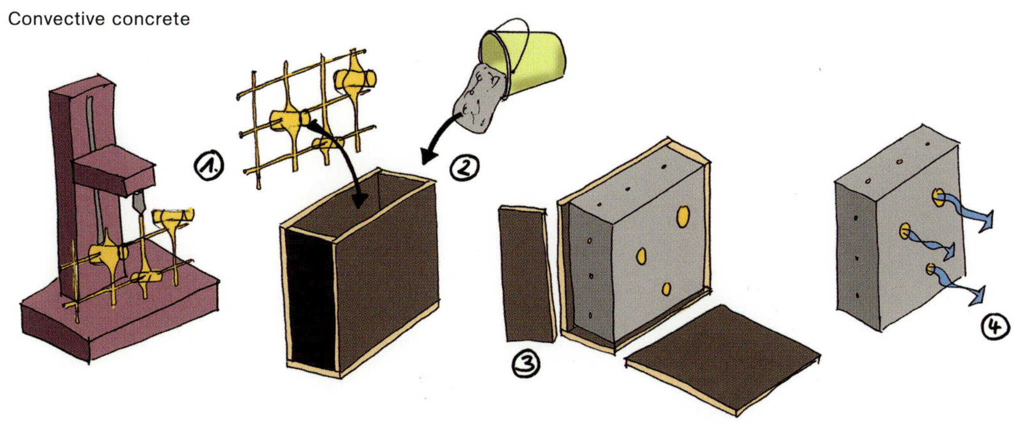

(1) Print advanced elements   **(2) Insert in formwork**   **(3) Demoulding**   **(4) Finished activated concrete element**

Activation of the concrete's core can be achieved by the use of customized formwork elements for a smart controllable active convection system in combination with advanced concrete mixtures. Additive Manufacturing (AM) is a good method for this kind of rapid prototyping because customized and free-form parts can be produced easily. AM of lost formwork differs from the approach of direct concrete printing. To benefit most from AM as production technology, the free-form and customized parts needed for the convective concrete will be printed.

To achieve an efficient convective flow, the embedded lost formwork and the concrete itself should function like a lung. The convection takes place with separate pipes on both sides of the concrete's core to increase the charge/discharge of the thermal storage process with the help of fans and valves. There will not be any openings through the slabs because that would cause thermal bridges. The concrete mixture with matching characteristics (density, porosity and lambda value) will be fabricated on the basis of computational simulations.

By integrating these additively manufactured smart voids and piping for convection within the customized concrete elements we are at the same time looking at the possibilities to compensate for the emissions from concrete production during the usage phase. With convective concrete the rate of carbonation, binding CO_2 within the concrete (CaO and CO_2 react to form CaO_3), can be increased. Carbonation is a known process that binds CO_2 to the concrete during the usage phase. Usually, only a thin layer near the surface will be able to bind the CO_2, but due to the internal piping in convective concrete, the surface area able to bind the CO_2 will increase significantly.

FREEFORM CONCRETE PRINTING: A HYBRID SYSTEM FOR FABRICATING COMPLEX CONCRETE GEOMETRIES

01-12-2015

IMAGINED BY Chris Borg Costanzi, Ulrich Knaack
KEYWORDS freeform concrete fabrication, concrete additive manufacturing, robotic control

The digital age has given architects the necessary tools to express themselves with unprecedented liberation. We are witnessing a new generation of architecture, one described by freedom of form and geometrical complexity.
The cost associated with producing concrete elements has a direct link to their geometry. Further cost is incurred if panels have variable thicknesses across their cross-section. These variations can take the form of edge returns in cladding elements (required for detailing), stiffening ribs (required for structure) or simply surface textures (required for architectural expression). In the context of free-form concrete geometries, fabrication of such features becomes even more difficult.

Robot arm combined with adaptable formwork

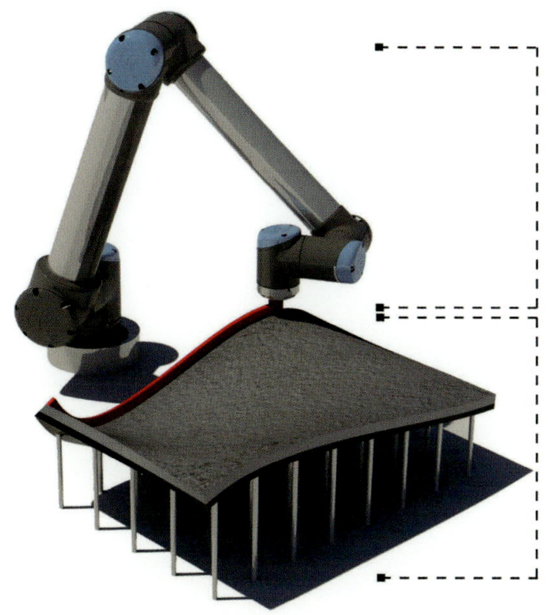

[2] 3D printing surface details.
Robotically-controlled printer automatically prints additional details (ribs, edge returns, surface textures etc.) on top of concrete surface without the need for complex moulds

[1] Concrete cast using flexible mould

Adjustable pin-bed used for casting double-curved concrete elements using a single mould. [Developed by R.Schipper]

Current molding systems for such elements are by no means cost-effective, as individual molds are still required for every unique panel. What is required is a more flexible approach to the fabrication of complex free-form geometries: a hybrid system of already existing techniques.

The proposed setup will be a combination of existing systems which includes flexible molding to cast double-curved panels of uniform cross-section and concrete Additive Manufacturing for the addition of surface details. The study will explore the possibility of efficiently fabricating free-form concrete panels with integrated edge details, ribs and/or surface textures.

1 Printed textures: Double-curve panel cast using flexible mold [grey],
   printed textures using a robotic arm [red]
2 Printed edges/ribs: Double-curve panel cast using flexible mold [grey],
   printed edge return using a robotic arm [red]. Structural ribs of greater
   height printed the same way. Material reduction through structural efficiency
3-4 Early tests: Extruded 'Schonox Q9W' on cast planar surface

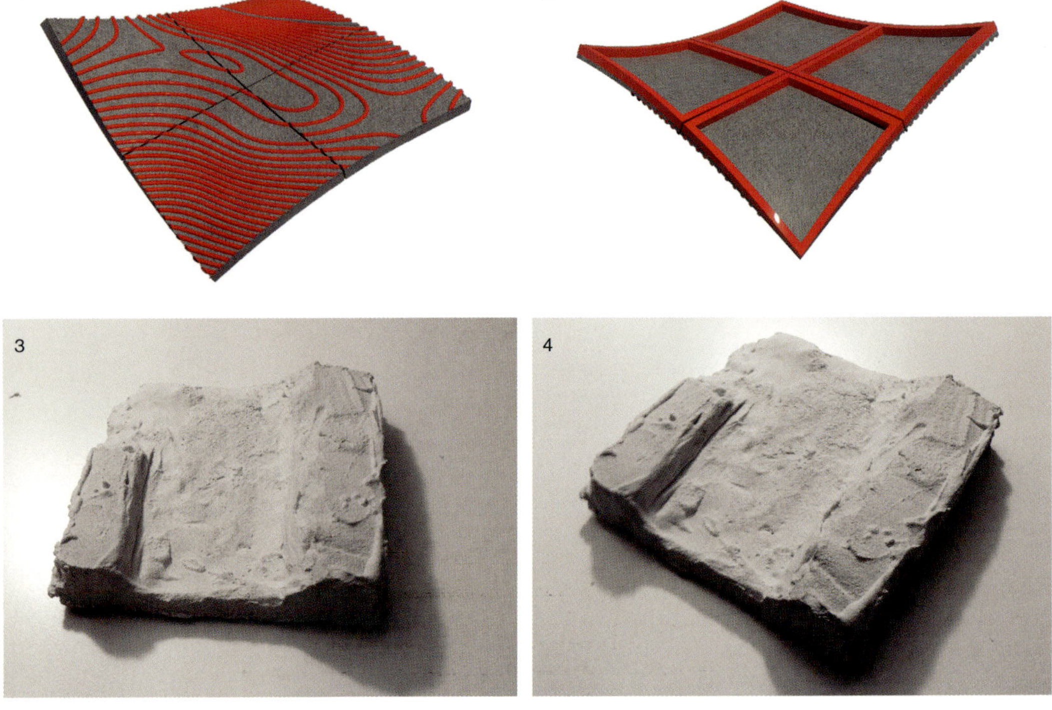

HYBRID BUILDING CONSTRUCTION
14-01-2014

IMAGINED BY Holger Strauß
KEYWORDS hybrid building construction, parts performance, construction sequence, materials selection, production process

Digital design often neglects the construction reality on-site.
Well-known materials and products rule the construction process and limit the possibilities at the same time. With the further development of materials and tools/production (e.g. Smart Materials, CNC technologies, etc.), the advantage of hybrid building construction came to the fore.
Now, new technologies have to be used to create the hybrid parts that are needed to combine "standard building construction and hybrid building construction". Parts need to offer added value in order to justify their application (cost, liability, risk, etc.).
Neither Lego® nor playdough alone is the preferred material/technology, but the hybrid building construction with new technologies, such as Additive Manufacturing, might be.

Hybrid Building Construction

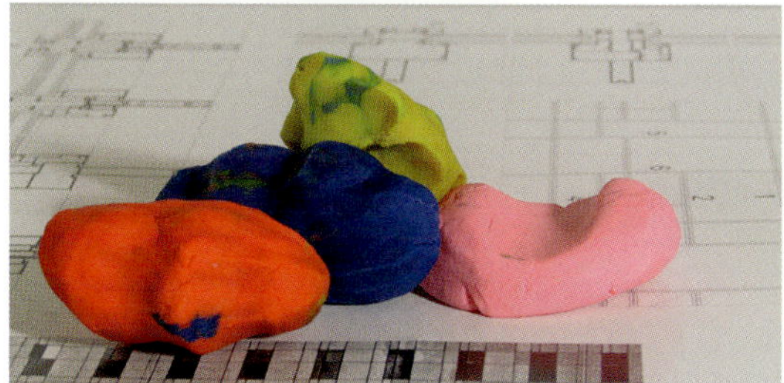

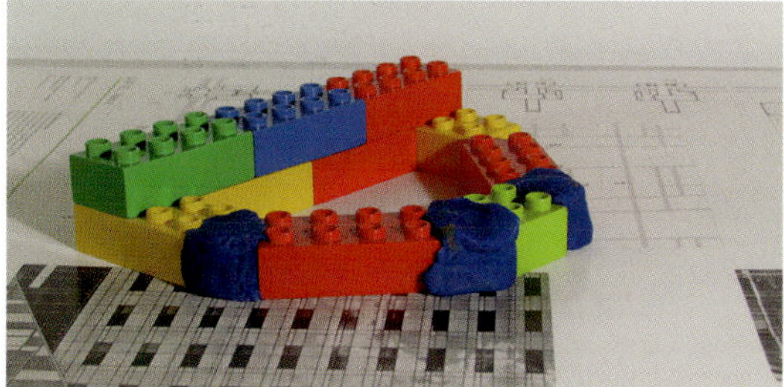

INTERACTIVE STRUCTURES
01-08-2015

IMAGINED BY Alamir Mohsen
KEYWORDS parametric nodes, interactive, form finding

The idea for this project was to build an interactive structure that acts as one unit.

Rhinoceros® and Grasshopper® were used to generate the structure elements. The definition allows the user to have full control of the structure as a unit by steering the fixed points toward any location, then controlling the location of every single point forming the whole structure.

The results will reflect the user's needs and vision. The definition grants geometrically generated connecting nodes with a list of the structure elements' lengths.

Different load conditions can be applied either to the whole structure or to specific points to check the stability of the overall structure.

The result can be easily manufactured by simply cutting the connecting bars according to the generated lengths, then 3D printing the connecting nodes.

Interactive structure

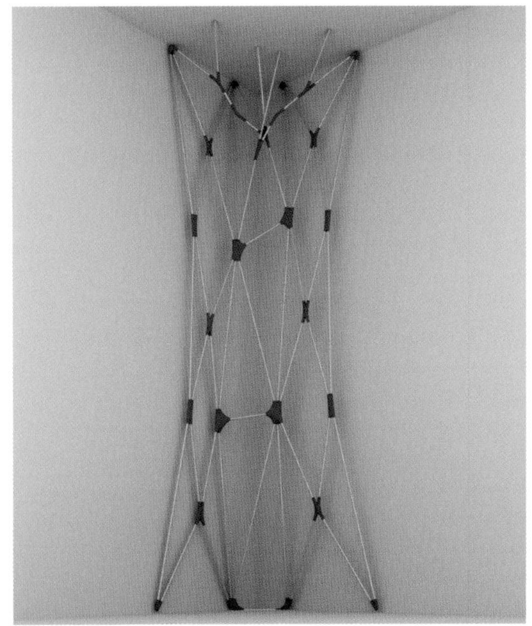
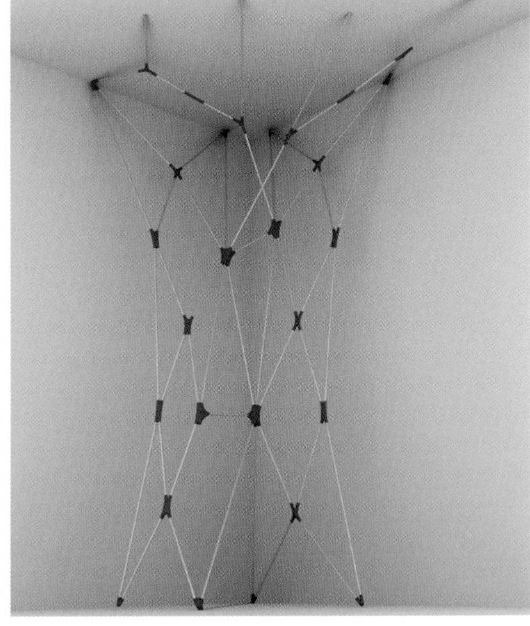

THE "SOFT" SPONGY SKIN
08-12-2015

IMAGINED BY Maria Valentini Sarakinioti, Ulrich Knaack, Michela Turrin,
Martin Tenpierik
KEYWORDS adaptive facade, integrated facade, cellular structures, PCMs, fluids,
sponge, dynamic system, heat storage

The main project is to design an adaptive facade system that is able to integrate
multiple functions in order to provide optimized thermal performance while being
applicable to a wide range of building shapes. Based on the geometry of cellular
structures and the system of the sponge, closed cells and movable fluid
accommodate insulation and heat storage where and when needed in the
building according to the indoor and outdoor conditions. The channels and the
pores of the facade allow water and other fluids to circulate throughout the
system in order to move the insulation and thermal mass from the outdoor side
of the facade to the indoor side and vice versa.

1 Principle of the soft spongy skin
2 Soft spongy skin
3 Soft spongy skin winter
4 Soft spongy skin summer

1

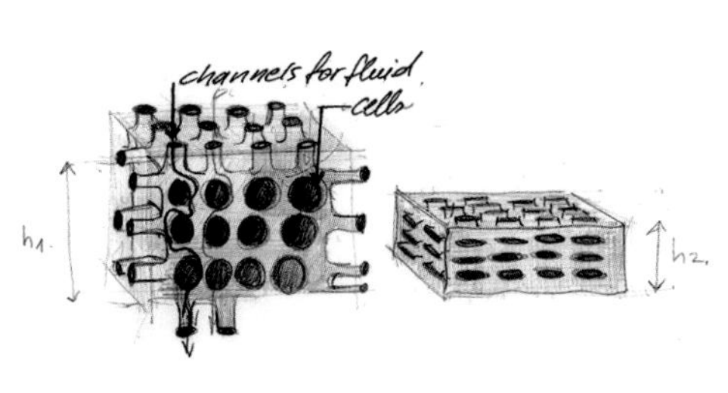

2

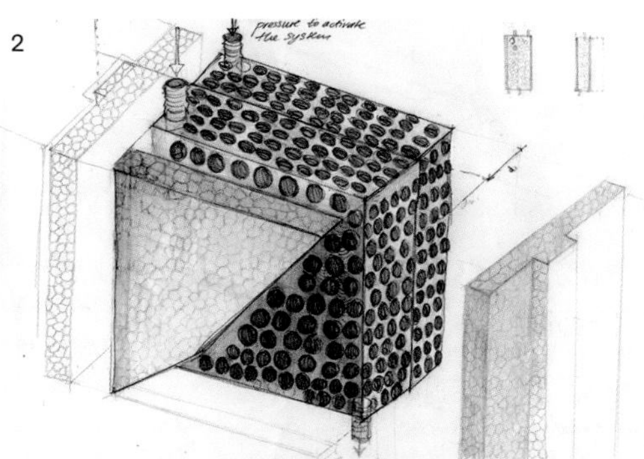

3

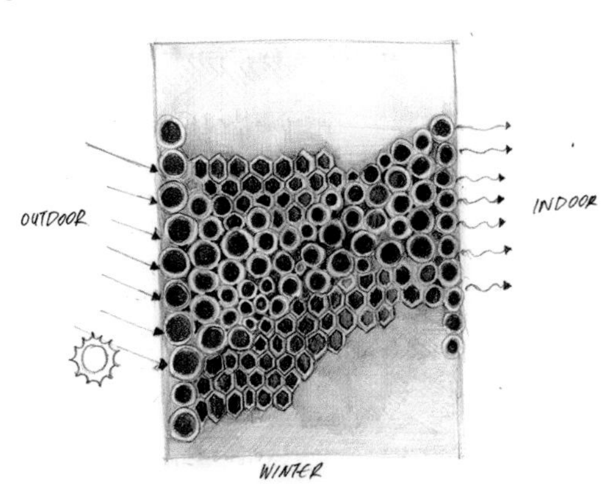

4

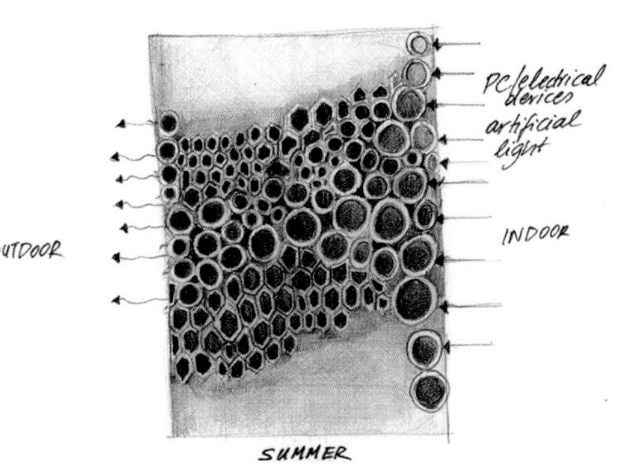

THE SPONGY SKIN

08-12-2015

IMAGINED BY Maria Valentini Sarakinioti, Ulrich Knaack, Michela Turrin, Martin Tenpierik
KEYWORDS cellular structures, integrated facade, thermal performance complexity, porosity, physical tests, experiment, thermal performance

The inspiration for this project originated in the cellular and porous structures found in nature and their complexity in shape. Additive Manufacturing methods can produce objects with high complexity in shape, material and functions that were not feasible before with traditional production methods. The main idea is based on the good thermal insulation properties of closed cellular structures. The product is a facade panel that contains polyhedrons and spheres of different sizes. According to the requirements for thermal insulation, load-bearing capacity and additional functions, these cells create parts with higher porosity and areas of higher density. The facade acts like a skin with strong and "soft" areas according to the conditions in each part of the building. The complexity is achieved with Additive Manufacturing methods from micro scale (cell structure) to meso scale (facade panel with variation in porosity) to macro scale (the spongy skin installed on a building).

1 Principle of the spongy skin
2-3 Spongy skin

1

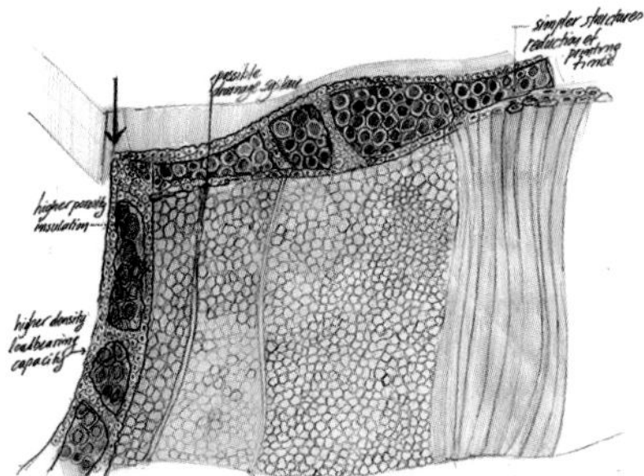

VORONOI FACADE
16-11-2015

IMAGINED BY Alamir Mohsen
KEYWORDS file-to-factory, parametric design, free-form, optimization

An optimized facade element was developed based on the Voronoi tessellation theory.

The idea was to figure out the lightest structure possible using the Voronoi tessellation's rules to come up with a new facade element. And as the requirement was to develop a three-dimensional free-form facade element, the results showed that the facade element has a diverse set of nodes.

The nodes were 3D printed because the nodes were not alike, which makes 3D printing an effective application.

The model consists of 37 different nodes with 65 bars and four supporting points, two fixed and two movable. The model was scaled to 1:20 and then built.

Voronoi facade

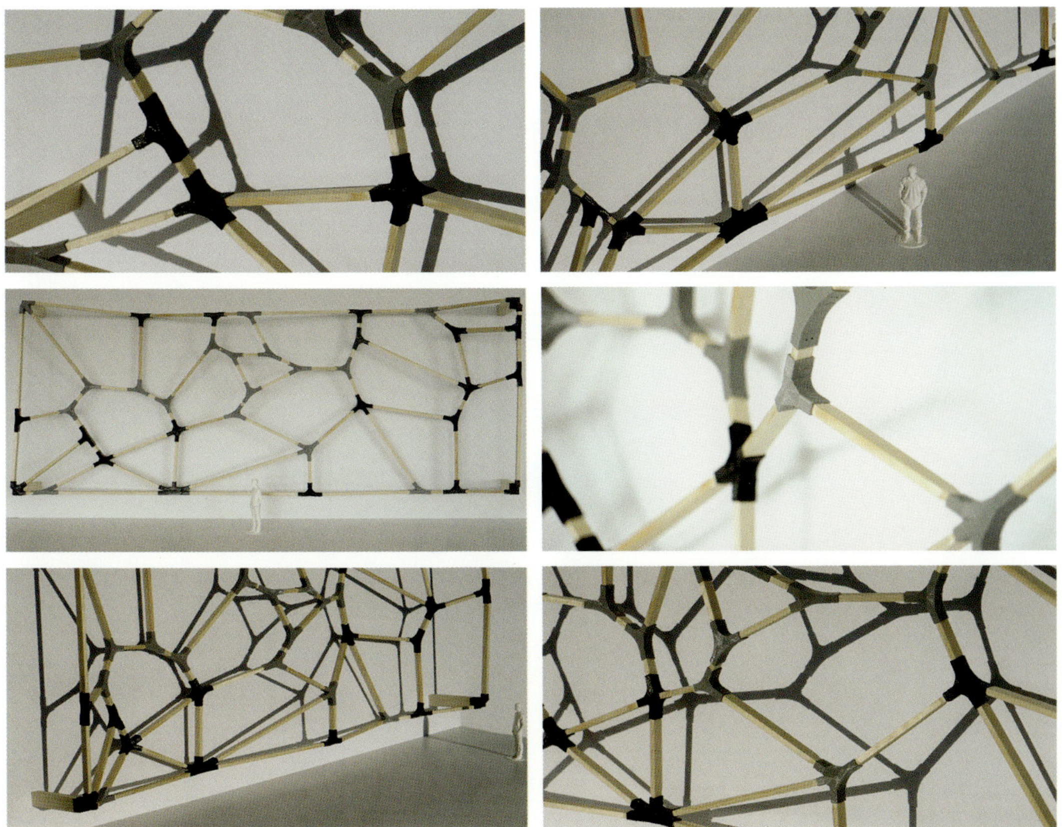

1ST GENERATION PARAMETRIC NODE N-AM 01 TO 08

01-01-2014

IMAGINED BY Alamir Mohsen
KEYWORDS parametric nodes, complex geometry, 3D printing

Complex geometries dominate today's architectural world; accordingly, we have to keep developing custom facade systems to accommodate these geometries. The process of developing custom facade systems tends to be time-consuming and full of challenges.

The idea behind this project was to try to develop parametric nodes for standard mullion and transom facades to overcome the problems. After several experiments, a ball connection seemed to be the most suitable solution to achieve the required freedom for the node to adapt to a wide variety of scenarios.

N-AM 01 (fig. 1) represents the first version, which is based on free ball connections that are fixated after certain angles were defined according to the specific geometry condition. Subsequent models called N-AM 02 and 03 (figs 2 and 3) seek to compact the node so that it is entirely embedded in the profiles. These versions proved acceptable geometrically but not structurally; which led to N-AM 08 (fig. 4), a structurally acceptable solution that increases the range of design freedom, making the node suitable for more conditions.

3

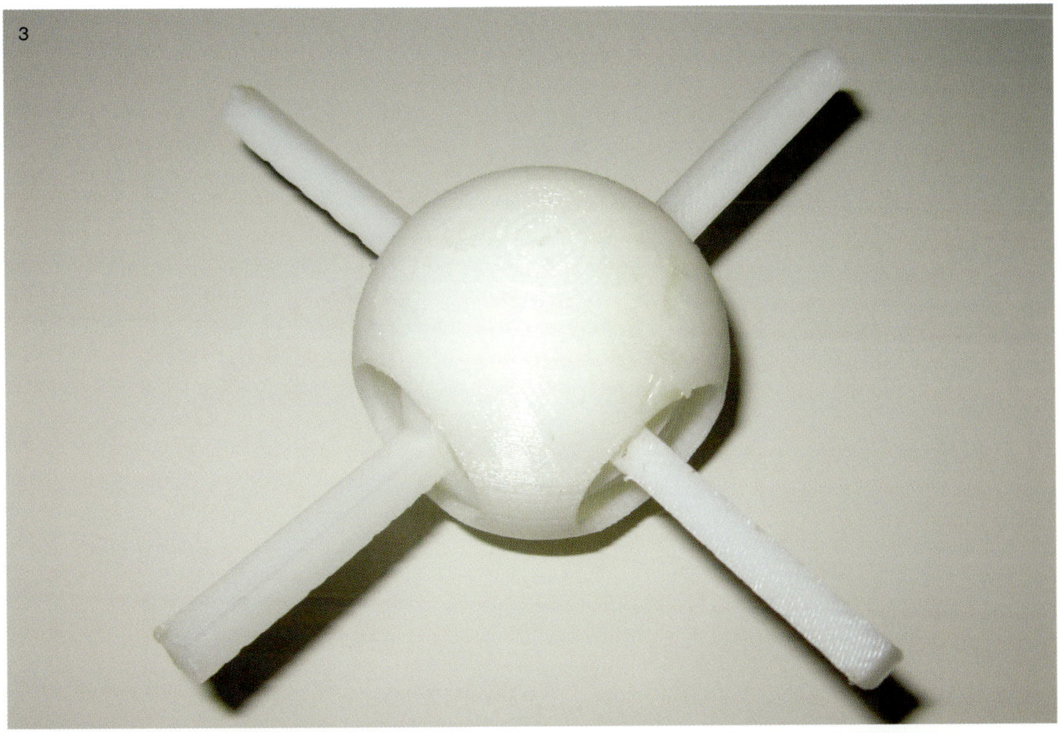

4

1 N-AM 01
2 N-AM 02
3 N-AM 03
4 N-AM 08

2ND GENERATION PARAMETRIC NODE N-AM 10

01-01-2015

IMAGINED BY Alamir Mohsen
KEYWORDS parametric nodes, complex geometry, 3D printing

The ongoing process of searching for the most feasible parametric nodes continues by taking a new route, which was to examine the compatibility of implementing 3D printing in steel combined with topology optimization approaches.

Digital parametric software allows us to generate a parametric node that can adapt to any geometrical condition.

The process started with utilizing form-finding algorithms (fig. 1) to identify the most appropriate form supporting the flow of forces. This was followed by a meshing process, which has a significant effect on the material subtraction process based on a topology optimization approach.

Then, a structural analysis (fig. 2) was conducted showing the exact location of the areas with the most and the least stress; the latter being suitable for subtraction without affecting the performance of the node.

N-AM 10 (figs 3 and 4) is the first prototype that was generated following the above-mentioned approach. The node was 3D printed in EOS stainless steel GP1 using the EOSINT M270 system.

The node properties are:
- Density 7.8 g/cm^3
- Tensile strength (as printed) in (XY) min 850 MPa, typically 930 ± 50 MPa
- In (Z) min 850 MPa, typically 960 ± 50 MPa
- Tensile strength (after heating at 650 °C for 1 hour) in (XY) typically 1100 MPa
- In (Z) typically 980 MPa

1-2 2nd generation parametric node N-AM (3D model)
3-4 2nd generation parametric node N-AM

1
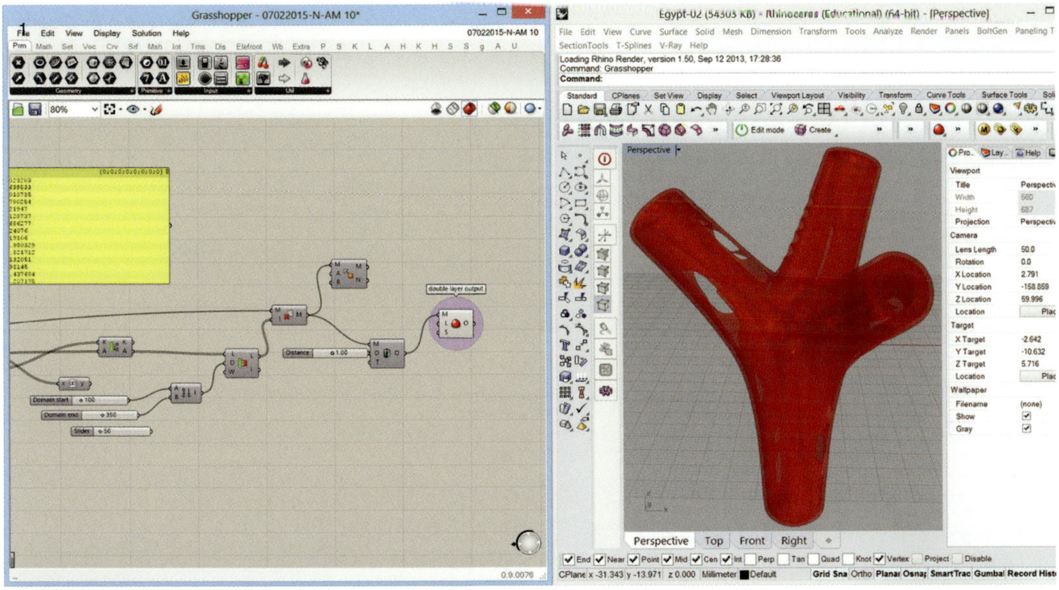
Grasshopper - 07022015-N-AM 10*
File Edit View Display Solution Help
double layer output
Distance
Domain start
Domain end
Slider
Egypt-02 (54303 KB) - Rhinoceros (Educational) (64-bit) - [Perspective]
Loading Rhino Render, version 1.50, Sep 12 2013, 17:28:36
Command: Grasshopper
Command:
Perspective
Top
Front
Right

2
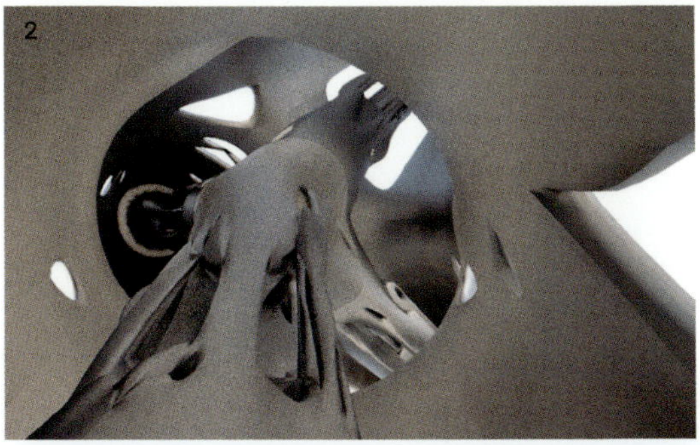

3
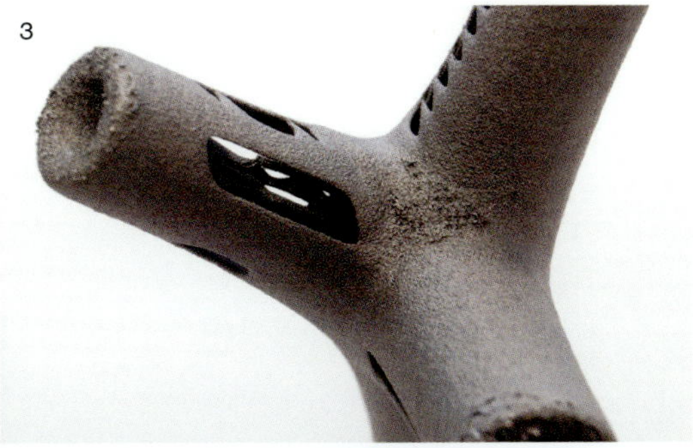

4

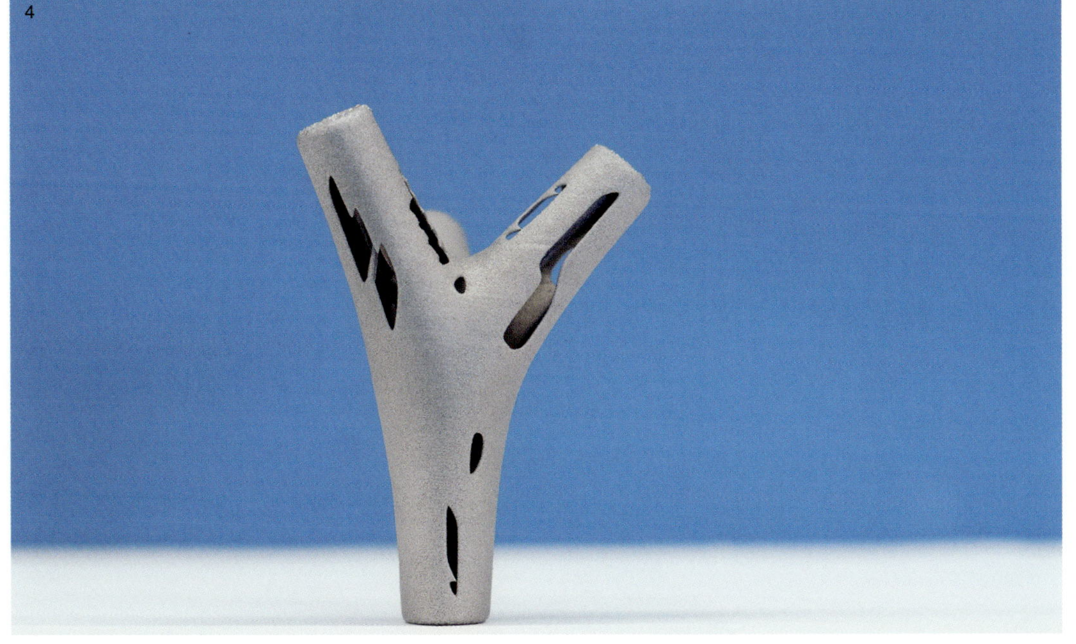

3D PRINTED FORMWORK FOR FREE-FORM CONSTRUCTIONS

02-10-2015

IMAGINED BY Alamir Mohsen, Sascha Hickert
KEYWORDS advanced formwork, concrete, optimization, free-form, curved wall, curved panel, file-to-factory

The basis for this idea was to bundle the individual competences of the ISM+D of TU Darmstadt. On one hand there was the DFG (German research funding organization) funded research project SPP1542 – "Light-weight building with concrete", and on the other, the research project "Parametrized topology optimization|3D Prototyping". The scope of the DFG research project included determining whether developing a formwork method for free-form facade panels is needed. The research work and discussions with the industry, architects and ready-made parts manufacturers highlighted another issue besides that of the already developed free-form formwork method. Joining the individual parts of a facade to create a high quality overall facade requires a so-called "edge return". Such a recess offers the advantage of stiffening the facade panels, and eliminates the need for an elaborate substructure and joining effort. With common formwork systems, this edge return is difficult and elaborate to accomplish.

Free-form wall

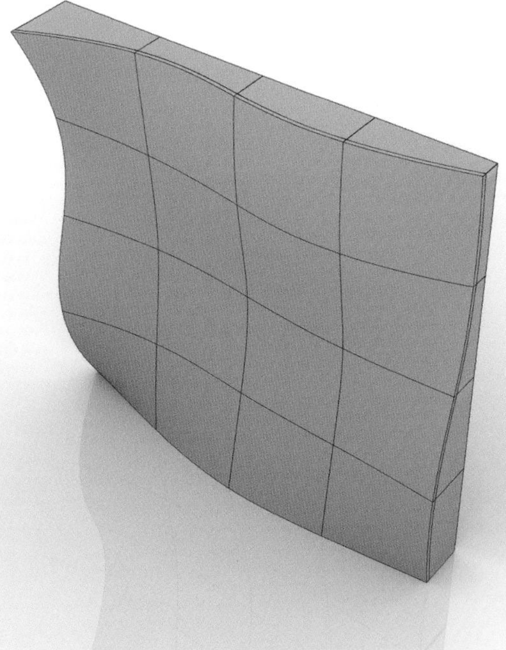

However, the idea presented here allows for a free-formed fair-faced concrete facade from mineral cast according to the "file-to-factory" principle in series production.

The current status of the project "3D printed formwork for free-form special constructions made from mineral cast for facades" is the prototype evaluation. A software element for the geometry was parametrized in the development environment Grasshopper® of the NURBS Modeler Rhinoceros®. First prototype formworks were produced on a scale of 1:4 (25 x 25 cm). Free-form facade panels with a parametrized, self-leveling edge return form the unique feature. Due to the parametrization it is possible to mount free-form facade panels on orthogonal walls without elaborate substructures. And the link to "file-to-factory" production offers a connection between the architect's or designer's planning software and the Grasshopper™ element, so that a facade design can be directly segmented and the appropriate formwork can be printed and concreted directly in the production facility of the ready-made parts manufacturer.

3D printed formwork

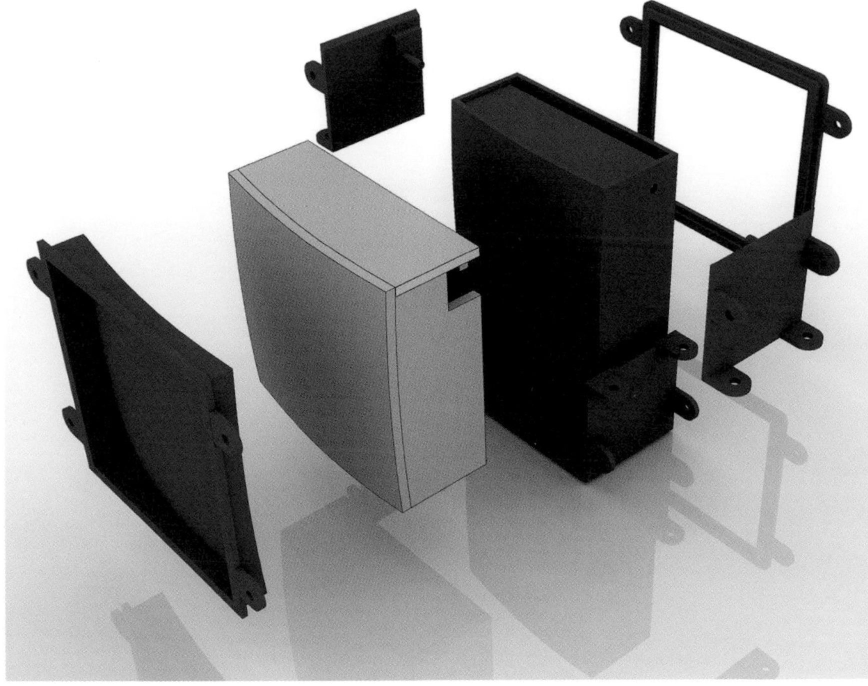

20,000 BLOCKS ABOVE THE GROUND
15-11-2015

IMAGINED BY Anton Savov, Ben Buckton, Jörg Hartmann, Sebastian Kotterer
KEYWORDS robotic fabrication, games, selective fusing, participatory design

Anyone can design a building in "20,000 Blocks Above the Ground" and have it
3D printed by our robotic arm Ginger. We use a game called Minecraft, which is
played based on simple graphics and rules. It is a game where you build and
demolish cubes of 1 x 1 x 1 meters. Currently about 22 million people use it.
First of all, we think about the rules of the game, we design the game and, as
others play, a model is designed.

The players are given a goal and insufficient resources to achieve it. To progress,
players must build shapes out of Minecraft blocks, choosing from an architectural
vocabulary defined by us. Players get rewarded with more resources for building
one of the shapes. While players compete to reach the goal, a building emerges
out of the shapes that they have built.

Minecraft model

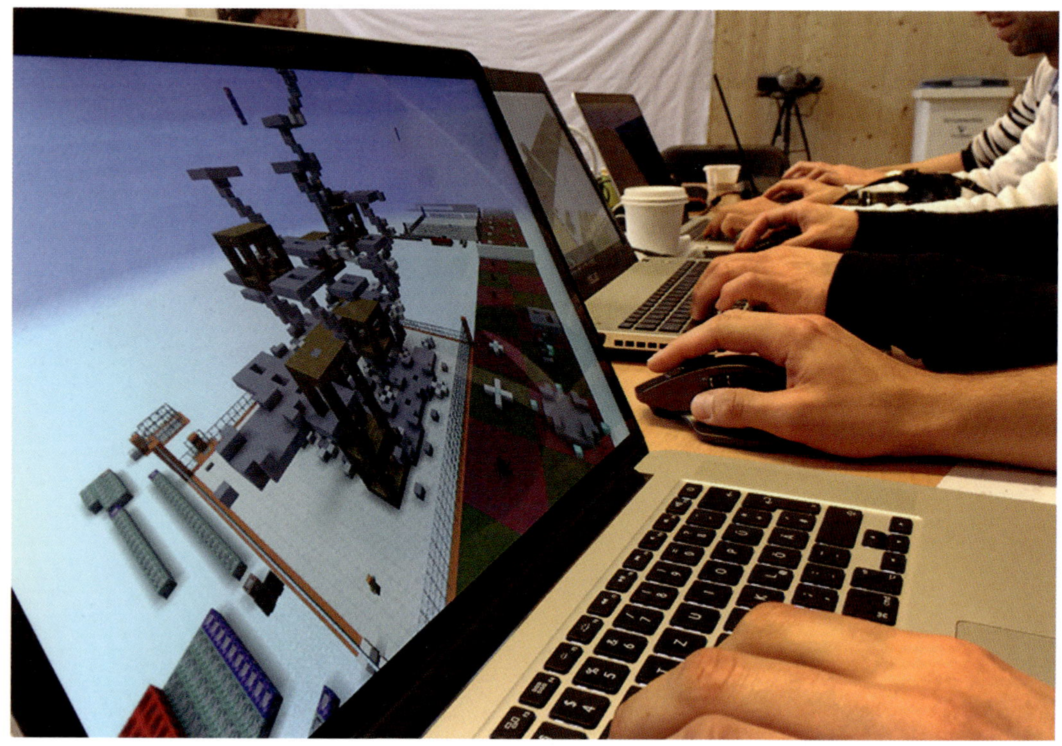

We then feed the point information for each Minecraft block to Ginger, which builds the model on a scale of 1:100. It grabs wooden cubes with a vacuum gripper, transfers them to the glue and then positions them exactly in the correct spot. If a cube is cantilevering, Ginger places freestanding cubes underneath it which are removed after the model is finished. This Additive Manufacturing process is similar to selective fusing of materials in a granular bed such as "binder jetting", with the difference that here the granules are a lot larger.

Principle of the 20,000 blocks above the ground

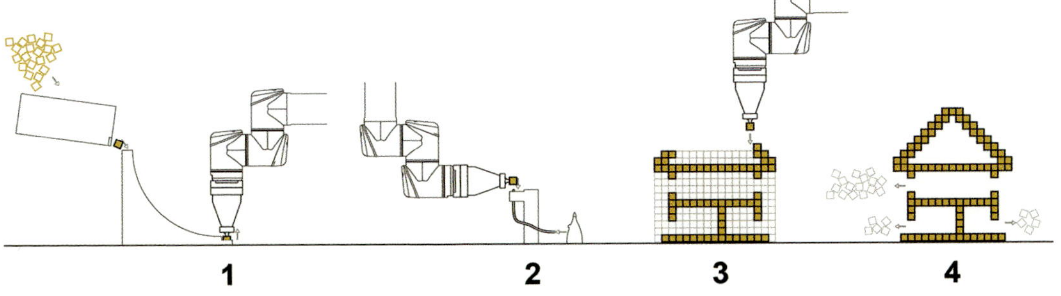

Stacking blocks with a robot arm

6. AM EXPLORATIONS

ADDITIVE WIRE
A LIVE, BREATHABLE HOUSE 3D PRINTED OUT OF MOSS
ANTI-ANISOTROPIC PRINTER
FORM-FINDING BY 3D PRINTING WITH VARIABLE ELASTICITY
HOW TO PROVE AM FOR BUILDINGS
INFLATABLE FORMWORK FOR MULTI-STAGE 3D PRINTING
MASSIVE SUSPENSION
POST PRINTING ASSEMBLY
REVERSIBLE COMPOSITES
SOFT GLASS SUPPORT
TENSION FOR ASSEMBLY
THE REAL GREEN PRINT
WAX ORNAMENT PRINTER FOR FORMWORK

ADDITIVE WIRE
09-12-2015

IMAGINED BY i10 workshop 12/2015 DDU/ISM+D
KEYWORDS magnetic field, redistribution, fibers, wrap

The additive wire process imagined here uses electricity to assemble small parts along a pre-spanned wire. First the parts float in a substrate without order (1). After feeding electricity into the wires the parts start to assemble (2). By a chemical process the parts are then fixed to the wire to achieve a stable bracing component (3).

Principle of the additive wire

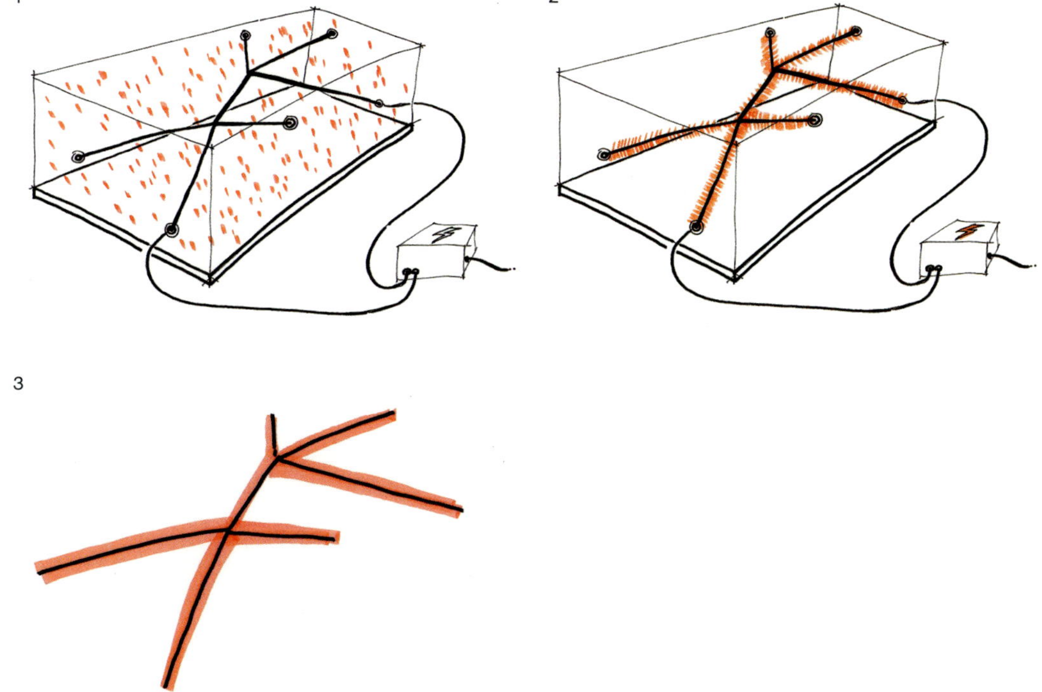

A LIVE, BREATHABLE HOUSE 3D PRINTED OUT OF MOSS
21-02-2016

IMAGINED BY Anton Savov
KEYWORDS sustainability, nature, swarm 3D printing

The organisms that moss is made of can survive mechanical intervention and
will keep growing just as before.
The moss can be mixed into a structural and nutrient paste of earth, fibers
and sand, and in turn the resulting paste can be used to 3D print a building.
It will take a few weeks until the moss regains its full life and grows all over
the new structure.
Once completed, the positive qualities of the moss walls such as filtering air and
malleability can be used for creating a better life environment for inhabitants.

Principle of a breathable house 3D printed out of moss

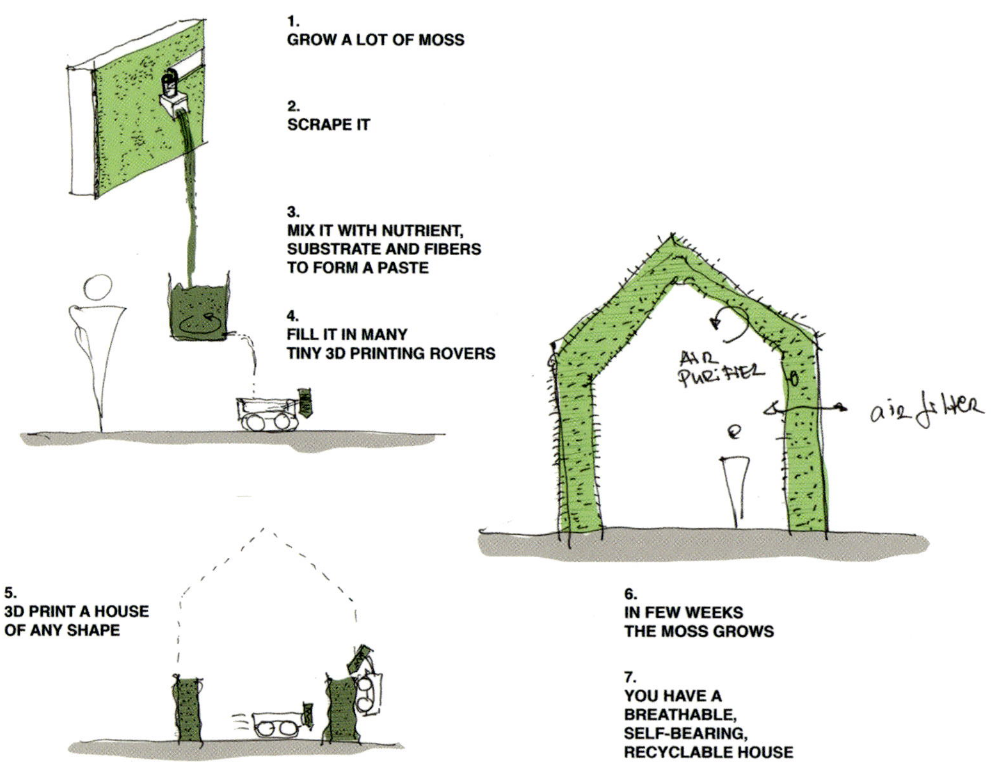

ANTI-ANISOTROPIC PRINTER
09-12-2015

IMAGINED BY i10 workshop 12/2015 DDU/ISM+D
KEYWORDS 3D printing, FDM, robotic arms, G-code

This idea derived from the necessity to use support materials when printing complex geometries that have inclined parts with angles of more than 45°.

3D FDM printers are controlled by what is called the G-code to control the movement of the nozzle in X-Y direction, while the build plate moves in a constant manner in the Z direction according to the thickness of the built layer. On the other hand, robotic arms have a decent freedom to move in all directions as well as to rotate about all axes.

Accordingly, the idea came up to combine the two technologies, which may lead to an end product that does not need any support materials to be printed regardless of the complexity of the geometry. This can be achieved by exploiting the advantage of the rotation movement that robotic arms can provide to allow the build plate or the piece itself to rotate in all directions and print the required part simultaneously.

To achieve this, a combination of the G-code of the 3D printer in XY and the G-code of the robotic arms for the rotation should be created with respect to the printing environment to achieve support-free prints.

Anti-anisotropic printer and print

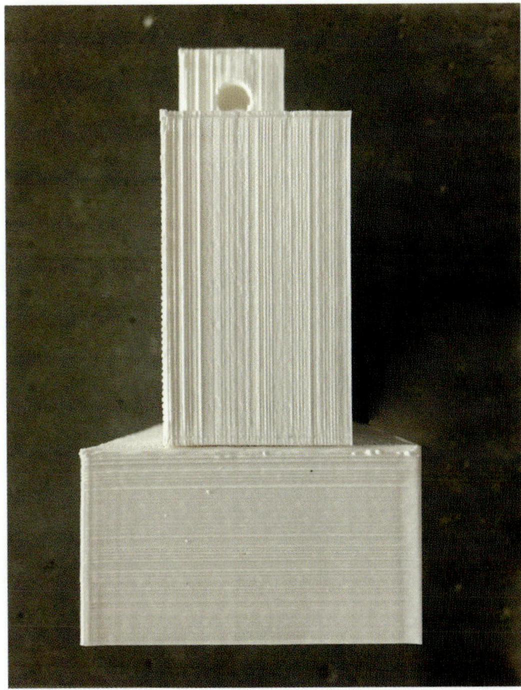

FORM-FINDING BY 3D PRINTING WITH VARIABLE ELASTICITY
09-12-2015

IMAGINED BY i10 workshop 12/2015 DDU/ISM+D
KEYWORDS material computation, 3D printing, elasticity

The fabrication method envisioned here needs an Additive Manufacturing process
that uses resin with variable elastic properties.
A vessel is 3D printed with a surface differentiated into elastic and non-elastic
zones. The vessel can be inflated to let the material compute its new shape.
It can also be used as formwork and filled with concrete.

Form-finding by 3D printing with variable elasticity

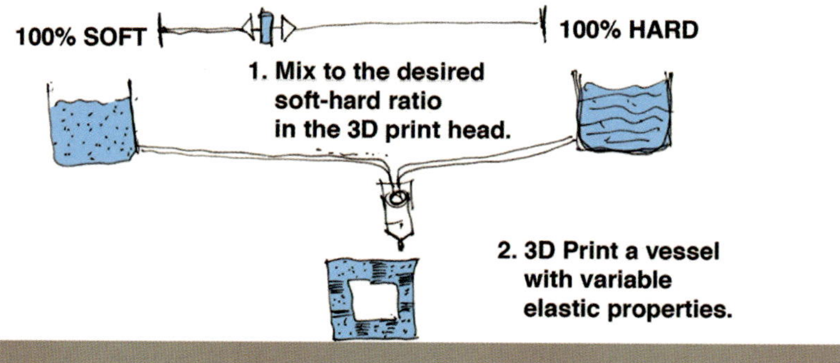

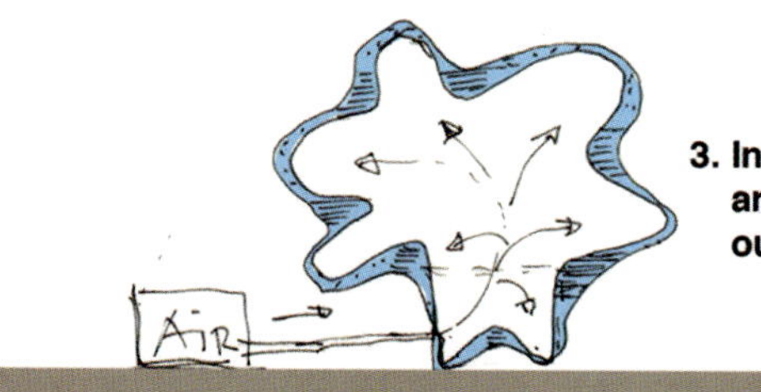

4a. Use as FORMWORK.
   Just cast concrete,
   plastic or similar
   on the outer or
   inner surface.

4a. Use as FORM.
   Just fix in this state with
   a chemical or thermal agent.

HOW TO PROVE AM FOR BUILDINGS
09-12-2015

IMAGINED BY i10 workshop 12/2015 DDU/ISM+D
KEYWORDS structural loads, isotropy/anisotropy, building material evaluation, computer tomography

When we suggest building with AM materials, the typical comment is that these materials are not known well and that the production process is still under development – correct comments. But in building construction we are very much used to dealing with the anisotropy of materials, a variation of possible load transfers and certainly with real force transport. Accordingly, we adapted our load and evaluation systems and added security factors for loads and material properties. This is what we could do for AM materials as well.

Consider the possibility to scan and screen each product made with AM, and to evaluate the isotropy/anisotropy of the object with a computer tomography scanner. Imagine this being just a normal process… It would ensure maximum quality on the material side – with limited factors to be added – and less additional material used. And if it becomes an established principle, prices for the methodology will drop dramatically; which means it could later be used for regularly produced materials as well – to improve security and quality.

Scan and screen additive manufactured product

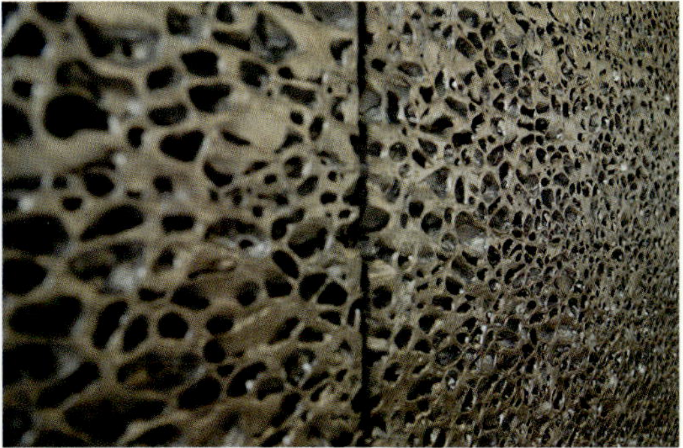

INFLATABLE FORMWORK FOR MULTI-STAGE 3D PRINTING
09-12-2015

IMAGINED BY i10 workshop 12/2015 DDU/ISM+D
KEYWORDS material computation, 3D printing, elasticity

An inflatable formwork made out of an elastic membrane is used as the basis for 3D printed domes or other structures. During the first stage, part of the formwork is covered with the 3D printing material to create a pattern on the surface. Then the formwork is inflated or deflated, and a new phase of 3D printing follows that uses the new shape as the basis.

Inflatable formwork for multi-stage 3D printing

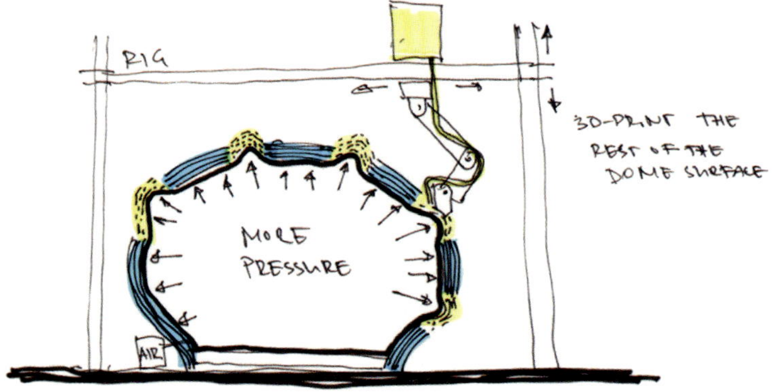

MASSIVE SUSPENSION
09-12-2015

IMAGINED BY i10 workshop 12/2015 DDU/ISM+D
KEYWORDS suspension, damping, massive, gradient, multi material, anisotropic

Multiple materials in different densities can be used to create a spring with a massive core. To do so, all materials need to be well connected to each other to deal with fatigue loads. If the materials are well connected such springs can be used for bridges. They will need less maintenance than conventional springs and can be integrated in the cables more easily.

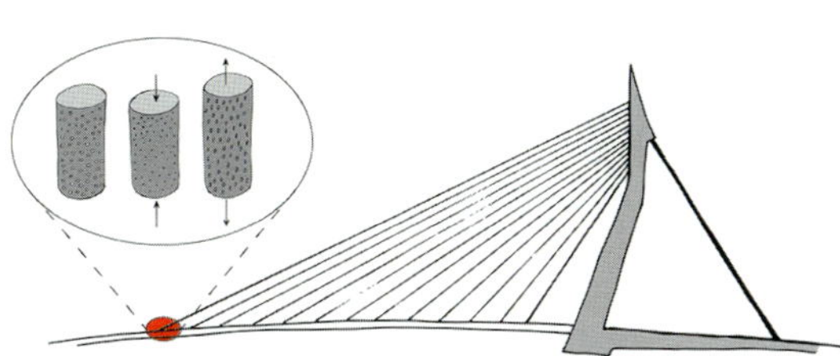

Massive bridge suspension principle

Erasmus Bridge

POST PRINTING ASSEMBLY
09-12-2015

IMAGINED BY i10 workshop 12/2015 DDU/ISM+D
KEYWORDS wrap, robotic shaping, material optimization

The robotic assembly process imagined here proposes an assembly of soft elements that change shape according to their positioning within the overall assembled system and the pressure applied to them (1).
In the second step the robot uses pressure-force sensors to measure the exact shape of the object and its elasticity (2).
In the last step the result is fixated by adding 3D printing material according to structural needs (3).

Principle of post printing assembly

1

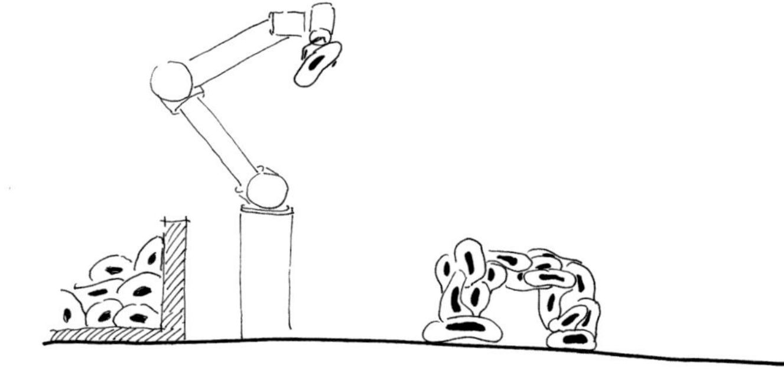

2

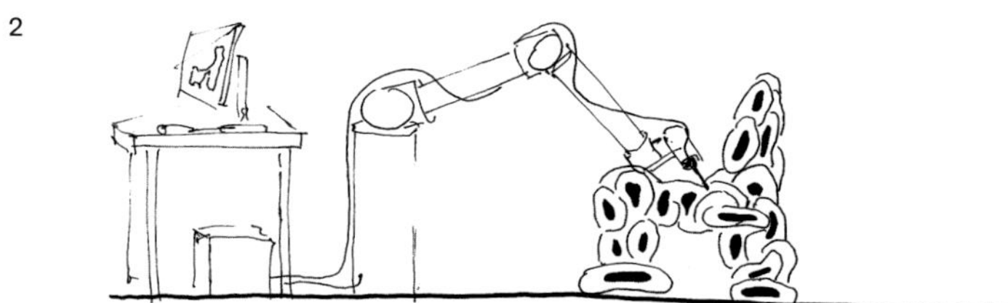

3

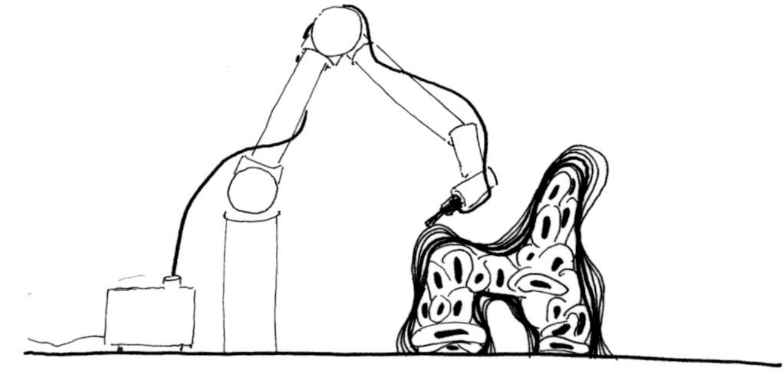

REVERSIBLE COMPOSITES
09-12-2015

IMAGINED BY i10 workshop 12/2015 DDU/ISM+D
KEYWORDS sustainability, composites

To make 3D printed buildings changeable and recyclable this method uses a reversible composite paste. This contains fibers to give it the desired structural performance and a soluble bonding agent to fix the shape in place. When a change is needed or a building has fulfilled its purpose, a solvent can be applied and the building returns to the original paste form. A new building can be 3D printed. Process steps:

1. 3D print a building with paste made out of fibers and soluble agent
2. Use the building until there is a need for major design change
3. Apply solvent and reconstitute back into paste
4. Print the new design

Principle of reversible composites

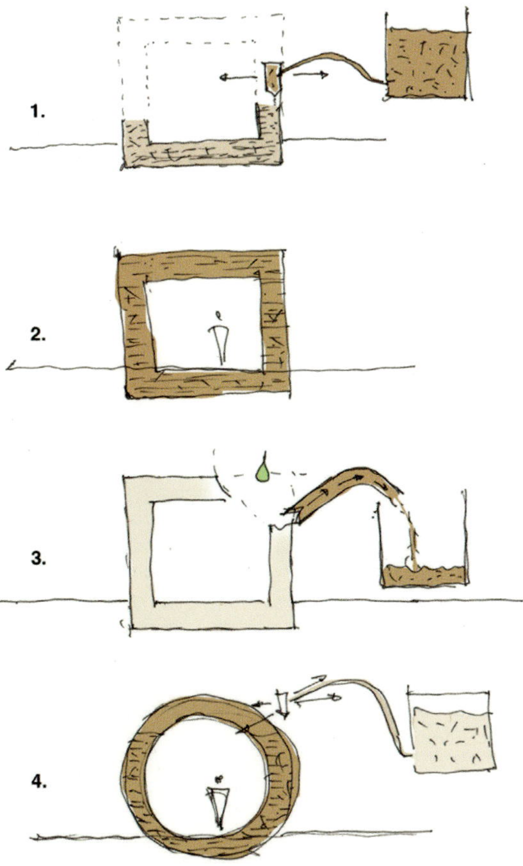

SOFT GLASS SUPPORT
09-12-2015

IMAGINED BY i10 workshop 12/2015 DDU/ISM+D
KEYWORDS glass, structural glass, graded materials, force-oriented structures

This is a realistic project: when using Tango materials, 3D printed materials of varying stiffness (shore stiffness), we can envision developing a structural support for glass, which allows collecting the leads from glass in a soft manner and then concentrating the forces toward the support structure.

This was actually the way it used to be in the good old times: mastic was used to cover and position glass in a steel structure. Due to its semi-flexible nature the mastic allowed the glass to adjust its position depending on the loads – while even avoiding load concentrations.
Nowadays, we concentrate the forces and are used to identifying the maximum load, which defines the dimension of the support and the glass. In addition, we also face the problem of tolerances: the edges of laminated glass are inherently not plan parallel due to the production process. This results in the problem of load implementation in only one glass pane, while the forces may be transported in both panes. The consequence being that unacceptable forces are to be accommodated by the lamination layer.

With the new concept of additively manufactured and graded glass support components we will be able to allow for a perfect fit for the support and, at the same time, a smooth implementation of structural loads into the glass.
And the nice thing is that it is indeed possible – we only need to investigate the how…

Soft glass support

Additive manufactured flexible material

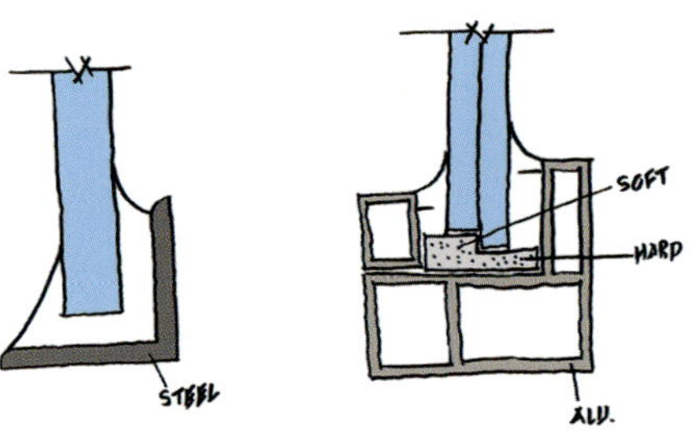

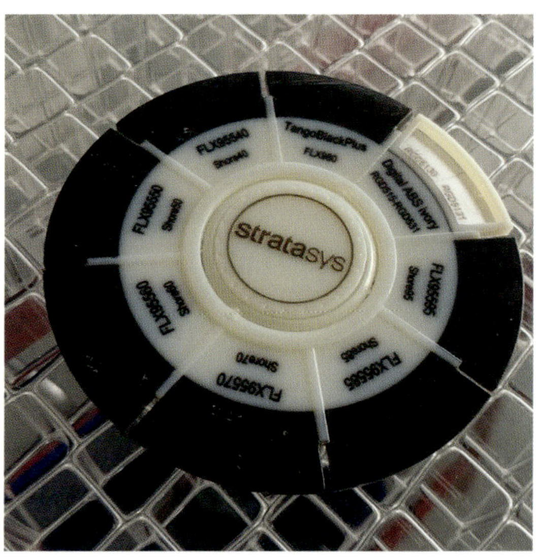

TENSION FOR ASSEMBLY
09-12-2015

IMAGINED BY i10 workshop 12/2015 DDU/ISM+D
KEYWORDS smart materials, pre-stress, smart components, interlocking

For complex component assemblies this process uses pre-stressed elastic
fabrics and building components that can be assembled by a simple movement
along a vector (1).
Instead of using the pre-stress in one direction only it proposes multi-directional
pre-stressing for the assembly of the components (2).
The idea is that the pre-stress is just used for the assembly and that the
components are designed in such a way that they fit into each other to create
a stable structure (3).

Pre-stressed elastic fabrics for assembly

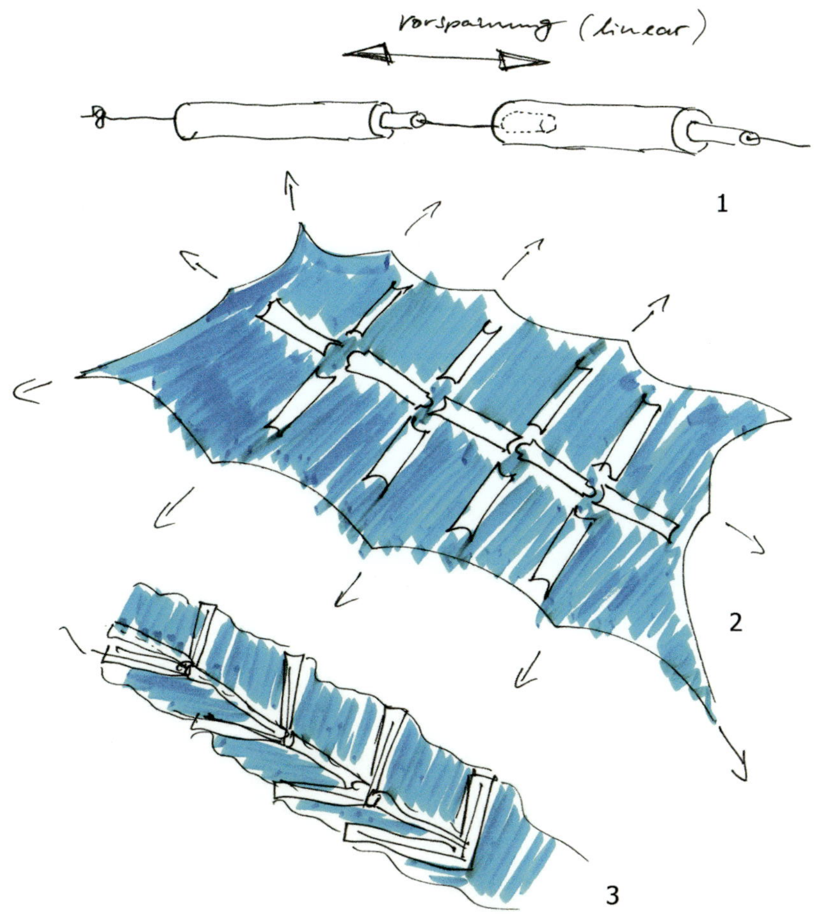

THE REAL GREEN PRINT
09-12-2015

IMAGINED BY i10 workshop 12/2015 DDU/ISM+D
KEYWORDS bio-printing, bio-adaptation, building with nature, trees

When trees grow they are able to adapt to conflicting physical components such as rocks, other trees or walls. Therefore, if we position components close to the growing tree, it will integrate these components in its growth and, with that, in its structure. Imagine placing load transfer components into a growing tree structure and allowing them to be integrated over time. The result will be an anchor point for forces that you would normally not be able to transport via a simple contact load transport. So we are able to acquire – through time and growing trees – construction components made of wood that are able to take structural stress forces.

And why is this printing? Well, printing means an additive method of assembling material – and this is what a tree does…

The real green print

WAX ORNAMENT PRINTER FOR FORMWORK

09-12-2015

IMAGINED BY i10 workshop 12/2015 DDU/ISM+D
KEYWORDS print on surface, wax, ornament, customization, standardized formwork

Printing with wax on standardized formwork allows us to customize wall elements. The printed wax will be washed off later.
Printing with multiple materials is another possibility. It could provide the option to print spacers for reinforcement bars and small ducts.

The concrete processing stays the same. Only additional features are printed on the formwork for a certain degree of customization within standardized formwork systems.

Principle of the wax ornament printer

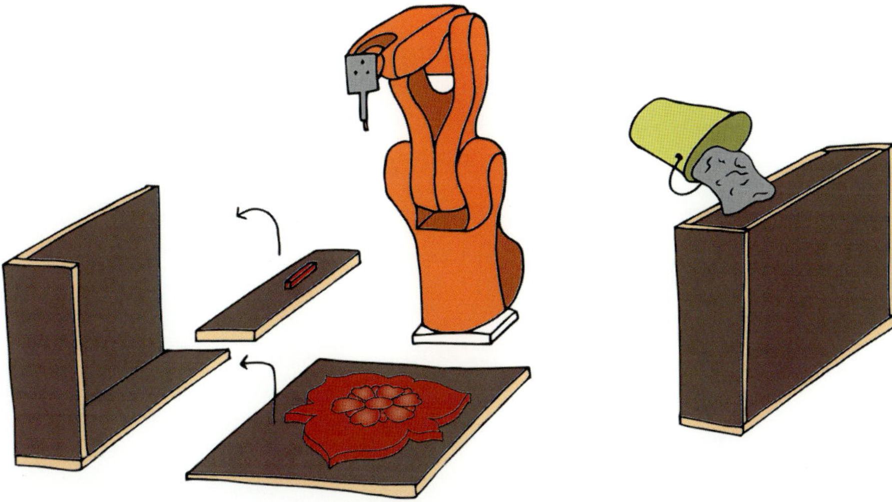

Ornament, Alcázar of Seville

7. WHAT A HYPE

When, in 2005, we began discussing the topic of Additive Manufacturing for the building industry people laughed at us. To specialized, too expensive, too much plastic… which might catch fire and thus cannot be used for building since our industry requires long-term fire resistance. Not to mention load-bearing capacity.

And today? There is an obvious trend toward building projects that are constructed in the form of a printed building, either in significant parts or in their entirety. And the desire to further incorporate the technology into building construction is growing – the bigger, the better.

Building and technology develop in waves: driven by the desire for development, societal, functional or design topics and/or technologies are picked up by planners and translated into new building projects. Next to improved performance in general, the goal is to create a stand-alone item, one that highlights creativity and thereby differentiates itself from others (which in itself is a performance…). In most cases, these waves develop from an impulse, a first project that focuses on a specific topic and addresses it with all possible consequences. Since it remains an unknown, high-risk terrain the executed projects are rather small, mostly experimental – and failure should not necessarily be viewed as a negative result but rather as an expression of the joy of experimenting and courage. The boundaries of the possible can only be extended if one dares to try. The projects are succeeded by interpretations of the technology or the topic – different points of view, technical options as well as economic parameters allow for developing a topic or technology that can be applied on a broader scale. This hype represents the peak of the development: the

technology is hot, hip, up-to-date – and is thus often copied. And this is the inherent source of the risk: copying brings with it ignorance, wrong applications and expectations that are too high. The result is disappointment – be it justified due to poor performance or unjustified due to high expectations, or simply the wrong application – the reason does not really matter. This phenomenon is followed by the phase of establishment – establishing true knowledge about the topic/technology and its potentials and possibilities. What does truly work, which applications make sense, who are the central players, and what does it all cost?

And as is typical, it all gets more complicated by overlapping issues – development waves overlap, occur at irregular intervals, have different cycles, amplitudes and effects. However, they do usually keep following the same pattern: peak, disappointment and establishment of the topic/technology in the building environment. Let us look at the field of facades, an environment very familiar to the authors of this imagine book; the last 20 to 30 years were dominated by the start of the development and subsequent elaboration of seeking increasing transparency, and thus research in the field of the material glass. Various techniques (point fixtures, pane dimension, load-bearing system, improved measurement tools) allowed for ever larger, uninterrupted glass panes – with a resulting higher degree of transparency. This topic was overlaid by energetic considerations of the building as a whole and the facade as an energy machine, in the shape of the double facade. Following the logics of integrating energetic functions in the building envelope, adaptivity – the possibility of adapting to function, climate and design – evolved into a separate focal point with regard to facades. In order to enable the integration of additional aspects and to use digital tools to their full design potential, a development evolved that could be called parametric; actually related to the structuralism of the last century, parameters are combined, and thus, quasi logically lead to an overall result. The trick in designing such a parametric lies in the preparation of the parameters and the process control during the development phase – a process that can also be viewed as a design process. And now, as a consequence of the parametric, we see ourselves forced to take a more integrated approach to answer construction related questions – integrated to a degree that we are not always able to actually build such components. Hence, a new manufacturing technology is needed – and this is where Additive Manufacturing comes into play: building parts can be created such that their functionality stands at the foreground. They are developed as monoliths, as building parts that can be produced in one manufacturing process with all sub-functions and components. Meaning we are in a phase of development of Additive Manufacturing.

This book certainly is part of the development. In 2010, imagine 4 – rapids was a first impetus; it showed the initial

approaches and was part of the development wave before the peak. In contrast, with this current book we are exactly in the phase of the peak: the topic is gaining importance in many areas, new developments in terms of materials, technologies and systems as well as design and functional concepts arise on a weekly basis, and the demand for real application in the built environment increases in terms of quantity and seriousness. It is only logical that we need to anticipate and consider the upcoming phase of disappointment and the related consequences.

As with all trends, certain groups of fans and specialists assemble. The latter are the ones that truly advance the topic by developing and communicating the topic/technology. This is where development happens. The fans, meaning those who are more concerned with the application of the topic or the technology, contribute less to the actual knowledge, but they do contribute by spreading the word – this is where the energy around a topic or technology is created that brings it to real application in the marketplace. This is where the hype evolves. Both depend on each other, sometimes they are represented by a single person, or by one person during different phases of the development – but the function itself

1

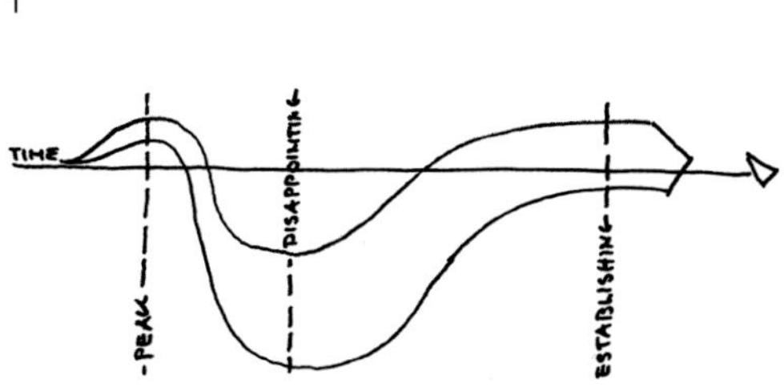

Development wave

2

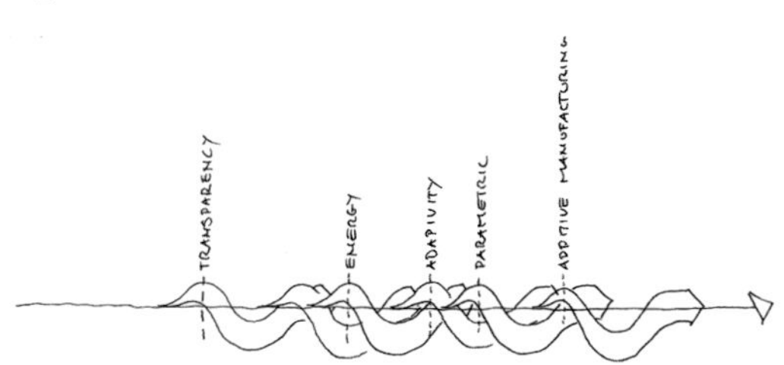

Overlapping development waves

remains the same: to develop and to promote.

With regard to the topic of this book, Additive Manufacturing, a group of like-minded people is in a phase of formation. The events concerning the technology are still events by and for specialists who are generally dedicated to technology. A broad transfer to the field of building is not happening – yet! However, establishment is not too far off. Lectures about Additive Manufacturing at traditional building events are still seen as exciting but exotic, somewhat unrealistic contributions – you need at least one visionary topic at each event, right? This too is an unambiguous description of a technology on its path to the peak.

How will the topic continue to develop? Naturally, the technology will advance – build size dimensions, precision and quality of the printed parts will increase, as will the homogeneity and stiffness in all three axes of the printed object. Speed and – logically – cost will be optimized when the technology is applied on a broad scale. Even though it is already being used in certain industrial areas, true building related application is still rare; mostly in the form of prototypes or one-offs. Besides cost and quality issues, one reason for this lies in the fact that there are still no approval methodologies, approval procedures or approaches for a building technical justification of the application. As with any good trend the early birds are the already described special solutions, single and special projects typically with dimensions and permissions customized to the project.

Thus, one central issue for the development of the technology in the building industry is to create binding systematics for materials and quality assurance as well as the dimensioning of building parts. With these steps and the corresponding engineering estimates as well as the safety levels and generally accepted tolerances common in the building industry, the technology would be fully applicable. It is utopian to expect this in the short term, however: the above described development cycles for transparency and the related topic of glass are far from completed – and as is common and necessary in science, each doctoral thesis opens up new, more in-depth questions that further increase the knowledge of the unknown. For the material glass, for example, this led various researchers and developers to form a group that advances the topic – and that will continue to develop it over the next decades, similar to the developments of other materials such as steel, concrete and wood. It is to be expected that the topic of Additive Manufacturing will play a major role of development in this field as well.

People such as Neil Hopkinson/ Nottingham are pioneers in the field – they recognized early on that the technology allows us to develop new approaches to solutions for known issues – and, in a secondary step, for new issues: legendary are the individualized sport shoes that Neil Hopkinson printed for himself after taking precise measurements of his feet. This illustrates the adaptation of the existing technology – extended with performance. Hopkinson also recognized the limitations of the technology, however: not everything must be printed; only the soles of the shoes are printed, the remainder is manufactured with conventional methods. And price and production time are critical parameters: here, the result of his work is the realization that from a particular stage in the development of equal components

3 Soccer shoe by Neil Hopkinson/Nottingham
4 Exemplary relation between production volume and cost for Additive Manufacturing according to Neil Hopkinson
5 Free-form facade node made with Additive Manufacturing (Holger Strauß with Alcoa/KAWNEER)
6 Free-form facade node made of standard aluminum profiles, cinema in Dresden by Coop Himmelb(l)au

onwards other manufacturing processes will be faster and more affordable – meaning that Additive Manufacturing makes less sense.

Building is one of the most individualized industries: even though our habits and function requirements do indeed show parallels, the location of a specific building with its climatic, geometric, formative and urban influences as well as the regional building cultural and craftsmanship oriented backgrounds are important factors that require an individualization of the built object. And while the individual components of the built object will remain the same – bricks are a good example – certain components will always be needed that need to be individually adapted to fulfill their intended function. Thus, in contrast to consumer goods, for example, building is a field predestined for individualization and thus for Additive Manufacturing.

Following this thought further, it becomes obvious that next to the individualization of the built object, it and its components could also be optimized in terms of technical and design aspects: the distribution of forces can be simulated and then implemented in the construction such that material use is optimized. In the same manner, bio-physical and structural questions such as drainage of facade profiles or self-locking joints of building components can be optimized too.

But against the background of Neil Hopkinson's realization about efficiency it is also evident that we should not print everything. Entire building structures or the desire to print any kind of complex mix of material combinations does not make sense even if the appropriate techniques were identified since cost and time would still cause limitations.

Thus, the challenge is to identify those components necessary for individualization and to then print them, while the other components can be produced with existing industrial processes.

Such individualized and optimized constructions offer the opportunity to construct in a goal-orientated manner: the construction is no longer defined by aspects of technical joining or the possibility to join components in general but rather by functionality in use. We will experience solutions changing from construction-oriented joining toward function-oriented construction – a paradigm change that will certainly be exciting.

In conclusion we would like to state that this development will afford a new type of construction-related company. Craftsmen are currently in the predicament of having to install industrialized components that in terms of technology require very little technical expertise – to facilitate assembly with low competence personnel and at low cost. In parallel, the development and investment cost for such components are too high for craftsmen companies to shoulder, meaning they will become dependent of the industry again. Additive Manufacturing with its capability of producing individualized building parts and/or connection nodes at relatively low cost offers the opportunity to return parts of the production chain to craftsmen companies – even though at the price that they develop the necessary competence to control the process. This is a field where a new craftsmanship could develop – a digital craftsmanship.

Naturally, the value lies in the building part/component being on site and functioning. But in terms of digital craftsmanship, production – or at least parts thereof – will be spatially separated from the system of construction: facade profiles will continue to be extruded in Turkey and shipped from there but the node solutions can be created locally. This offers a nice analogy to Konrad Wachsmann: in his world of thinking it is no longer the industrially manufactured item that is the one-of-a-kind object but rather the machine fabricating the product. Translated into the technology of Additive Manufacturing – logically this is also true for subtractive methods – the data record is the original from which any number of clones can be created.

Against the background of the above, it is the strategy of the contributors to this book to concern themselves with the various developing technologies and materials of Additive Manufacturing and to make them usable in the building industry. Which materials can be sensibly used in terms of the technical and economic requirements in the building world? What are the estimates for durability and material parameters when considering the long lifetime cycles of buildings? How can this technology be integrated into the building processes? However, the most exciting question concerns what the buildings will look like. In how far will design and functions alter, and will the buildings be better, whatever the definition of "better" might be?

What a hype – yes, free-form constructions indeed suggest themselves as a direct goal for the new technologies since we still do not have adequate solutions for the structural question of how to construct free-form buildings, and continue to solve this problem with clad skeleton constructions. But it is more exciting and certainly more important in the long term to discuss how we can transfer this technology – Additive Manufacturing – to standard constructions with a necessary degree of individualization. Therefore, the issue is less about one-offs but rather about a general applicability and validity for building construction.

APPENDIX

CVs

ULRICH KNAACK (*1964) was trained as an architect at the RWTH Aachen in Germany. After earning his degree, he worked at the university as a researcher in the field of structural use of glass and completed his studies with a PhD degree.

In his professional career Knaack worked as an architect and general planner in Düsseldorf, Germany, winning several national and international competitions. His projects include high-rise and offices buildings, commercial buildings and stadiums.
In his academic career Knaack was professor of Design and Construction at the University of Applied Sciences in Detmold, Germany. He also was and still is appointed professor for Design of Construction at Delft University of Technology (Faculty of Architecture), Netherlands where he developed the Facade Research Group. In parallel, he is professor of Facade Technology at TU Darmstadt (Faculty of Civil Engineering), Germany, where he participates in the Institute of Structural Mechanics + Design.

He organizes interdisciplinary design workshops and symposiums in the field of facades and is author of several well known reference books, articles and lectures.

DENNIS DE WITTE (*1988) completed his Master degree in Building Technology at Delft University of Technology, Netherlands in 2015, upon which he became a research associate under the supervision of Prof. Ulrich Knaack in Germany. To obtain his doctoral degree at TU Darmstadt, Faculty of Civil Engineering, he is investigating ways of implementing additively manufactured ceramic components within the built environment.

During his studies he was already involved in education and, over the past two years, worked as student assistant at the University, chair of Design of Construction. In parallel to his work in Darmstadt he continued working part time on research into additive manufacturing in Delft.

Simultaneously working at both universities, his research on "how materials and additive production processes match and how a variety of products perform within our built environment" continues.

ALAMIR MOHSEN (*1986) obtained his Bachelor degree in architecture from Ain Shams University in Cairo, Egypt in 2007; later on he worked as technical architect for an Egyptian construction company (Wady el Nile) in Cairo besides being a designer for an Egyptian consultant (Pioneer, Consultant, Design & Urban). In 2009 he moved to an international architectural consultant (Dar el Handasa) based in Cairo. The following four years he was involved in several projects in the Middle East and Africa.

In 2014 he earned his Master degree in facade engineering at the University of Applied Sciences in Detmold, Germany. Since then he has been working on his PhD study at TU Darmstadt entitled "N-AM| The Imminent Future of Parametric Nodes" and as research assistant under the supervision of Prof. Ulrich Knaack. He also works as a facade engineer in the parametric department at Bollinger + Grohmann engineering office in Frankfurt, Germany. Since 2013 he has worked as a writer for the scientific blog www.facadeworld.com.

OLIVER TESSMANN (*1973) is professor at TU Darmstadt where he is heading the Digital Design Unit (DDU) at the Faculty of Architecture. His teaching and research revolves around computational design and digital fabrication in architecture.

From 2012 until 2015 he was assistant professor (tenure track) at the School of Architecture and the Built Environment, KTH Stockholm. He has been a guest professor at Staedelschule Architecture Class (SAC) in Frankfurt, heading the specialization "Architecture and Performative Design". He worked with the engineering office Bollinger + Grohmann in Frankfurt at the interface between architecture and engineering. After graduating in 2001 from the University of Kassel, Germany, he worked with Coop Himmelb(l)au in Mexico and Vienna and Bernhard Franken in Frankfurt. In 2008, Oliver Tessmann received a doctoral degree after four years of research in the field of "Collaborative Design Procedures for Architects and Engineers" at the University of Kassel. The research sought novel strategies for using structural analysis as a design driver in architecture by establishing digital interfaces between the disciplines. His work has been published and exhibited in Europe, Asia and the US.

MARCEL BILOW (*1976) studied architecture at the University of Applied Science in Detmold, Germany, completing his studies with honors in 2004. During this time, he also worked at several architectural offices, focusing on competitions and later on facade planning. Simultaneously, he and Fabian Rabsch founded the architectural office "raum204". After graduating, he worked as a lecturer and became head of research and development at the chair of Design and Construction at Detmold School of Architecture and Interior Architecture under the supervision of Prof. Ulrich Knaack. Since 2005, he has been a member of the Facade Research Group at Delft University of Technology (Faculty of Architecture), Netherlands and in 2012 he became head of the facade prototype course, the Bucky Lab. That same year he completed his PhD thesis on climate related facade studies.

REFERENCES

ASTM International. (2012). ASTM F2792 — 12a: *Terminology for Additive Manufacturing Technologies* (Withdrawn 2015). Conshohocken, PA: ASTM

Carpo, M. (2011). *The Alphabet and the Algorithm*. Cambridge: MIT Press

de Witte, D. (2015). *Concrete in an AM process: Freeform concrete processing*. (M.Sc.), Delft: TU Delft

Fastermann, P. (2012). 3D-Druck/Rapid Prototyping. *Eine Zukunftstechnologie-kompakt erklärt*. Berlin: Springer-Verlag

Fischer, T. (2008). *Designing (tools (for designing (tools (for ...))))*. D.Phil, RMIT University

Fromm, A. (2014). *3-D-Printing zementgebundener Formteile: Grundlagen, Entwicklung und Verwendung*. (Dr.-Ing.), Kassel: Kassel University Press

Gebhardt, A. (2011). *Understanding Additive Manufacturing: Rapid Prototyping – Rapid Tooling – Rapid Manufacturing*. Munich: Carl Hanser Verlag

Gibson, I., Rosen, D.W. & Stucker, B. (2015). *Additive Manufacturing Technologies: Rapid Prototyping to Direct Digital Manufacturing* (2nd ed.). New York: Springer

Hansmeyer, M. (2016). "Michael Hansmeyer-Computational Architecture". Retrieved from http://www.michael-hansmeyer.com/

Knaack, U., Klein, T. & Bilow, M. (2013). *Imagine 04: Rapids*. Rotterdam: nai010 publishers

Lim, S., Buswell, R.A., Le, T.T., Austin, S.A., Gibb, A.G. & Thorpe, T. (2012). "Developments in construction-scale additive manufacturing processes". *Automation in Construction*, 21, pp. 262-268. doi:10.1016/j.autcon.2011.06.010

Mcor Technologies (2016). "3D Printing and Rapid Prototyping". Retrieved from http://mcortechnologies.com/

Morel, P. (n.d.). "Betonguss". Retrieved from http://www.voxeljet.de/case-studies/case-studies/betonguss-mit-sandformen/

Peters, B. (2013). "Computation Works: The Building of Algorithmic Thought". In *Architectural Design*, 83(2), pp. 8-15. doi:10.1002/ad.1545

Peters, T. (2015). "Suddenly the ornament is free". *MARK*, 58, Oct/Nov 2015

Reiser, J. & Umemoto, N. (2006). *Atlas of Novel Tectonics*. New York: Princeton Architectural Press

Ren, S. & Galjaard, S. (2015). "Topology Optimisation for Steel Structural Design with Additive Manufacturing". In R.M. Thomsen, M. Tamke, C. Gengnagel, B. Faircloth & F. Scheurer (eds), *Modelling Behaviour: Design Modelling Symposium 2015* (pp. 35-44). Cham (CH): Springer International Publishing

Reyner Banham, P. (1969). *Architecture of the Well-tempered Environment*. Chicago: The University of Chicago Press

Schöpf, G. (2015). *Additive Fertigung: Der Fachbereich für Rapid Prototyping,-Tooling,-Manufacturing*, 10/2015. Retrieved from http://www.x-technik.at/fachbereiche/additive_fertigung.php

Strauß, H. (2013). *AM Envelope: The potential of Additive Manufacturing for facade constructions*. (PhD.), Delft: TU Delft

Tam, K.-M.M., Coleman, J.R., Fine, N.W. & Mueller, C.T. (2015). *Stress line additive manufacturing (SLAM) for 2.5-D shells*. Paper presented at Future Visions, Amsterdam

Thompson, D'A.W. & Albus, A. (2006). *Über Wachstum und Form*. Frankfurt am Main: Eichborn Verlag

Wachsmann, K. (1959). *Wendepunkt im Bauen* (vol. 160). Wiesbaden: Otto Krauskopf Verlag

Zaera-Polo, A. (2009). "Patterns, Fabrics, Prototypes, Tessellations". *Architectural Design*, 79(6), pp. 18-27

ALSO PUBLISHED

- Imagine 01 – Façades
  ISBN 978-90-6450-656-7
- Imagine 02 – Deflateables
  ISBN 978-90-6450-657-4
- Imagine 03 – Performance Driven Envelope
  ISBN 978-90-6450-675-8
- Imagine 04 – Rapids
  ISBN 978-90-6450-676-5
- Imagine 05 – Energy
  ISBN 978-90-6450-761-8
- Imagine 06 – Reimagining the Envelope
  ISBN 978-90-6450-800-4
- Imagine 07 – Reimagining Housing
  ISBN 978-94-6208-036-2
- Imagine 08 – Concretable
  ISBN 978-94-6208-221-2
- Imagine 09 – prototyping efnMOBILE
  ISBN 978-94-6208-291-5

CREDITS

IMAGINE 10 – RAPIDS 2.0

Series on technology and material development, Chair of Design of Construction at Delft University of Technology.

Imagine provides architects and designers with ideas and new possibilities for materials, constructions and facades by employing alternative or new technologies. It covers topics geared towards technical developments, environmental needs and aesthetic possibilities.

ILLUSTRATION CREDITS

Page 20-4TU.Bouw AM Workshop: Gevel 2016-Ahoy. Image courtesy of 4TU.Bouw Page 40-3D printed lightweight concrete. Image courtesy of Klaudius Henke

All other illustrations are made available by the authors and people who contributed to this book, or as mentioned in the image description.

www.nai010.nl

ISBN 978-94-6208-293-9

Available in North, South and Central America through D.A.P./Distributed Art Publishers Inc, 155 Sixth Avenue 2nd Floor, New York, NY 10013-1507, tel +1 212 627 1999, fax +1 212 627 9484, dap@dapinc.com. Available in the United Kingdom and Ireland through Art Data, 12 Bell Industrial Estate, 50 Cunnington Street, London W4 5HB, tel +44 208 747 1061, fax +44 208 742 2319, orders@artdata.co.uk

SERIES EDITORS

Ulrich Knaack, Tillmann Klein, Marcel Bilow

PEER REVIEW

Marco Hemmerling, Thomas Auer

AUTHORS

Ulrich Knaack, Dennis de Witte, Alamir Mohsen, Marcel Bilow, Oliver Tessmann

TEXT EDITING

Usch Engelmann, John Kirkpatrick

DESIGN

Studio Minke Themans i.c.w. Marieke Bokelman

PRINTED BY

Wilco, Amersfoort

PARTICIPANTS i10 WORKSHOP 12/2015 DDU/ISM+D

Dennis de Witte, Carina Kisker, Ulrich Knaack, Alamir Mohsen, Anton Savov, Alexander Stefas, Oliver Tessmann, Bastian Wibranek